Campaign to Protect
Rural England

A PORTRAIT OF ENGLAND

EDITED BY JOANNA EEDE

SUPPORTED BY

CALOR

THINK
BOOKS

A Think Book

First published in Great Britain in 2006 by
Think Publishing
The Pall Mall Deposit
124-128 Barlby Road, London W10 6BL
www.think-books.com

Published in association with
The Campaign to Protect Rural England
128 Southwark Street, London SE1 0SW
www.cpre.org.uk
Registered Charity Number 1089685

Distributed in the United States and Canada by
Sterling Publishing Co., Inc.
387 Park Avenue South
New York, NY 10016-8810

Design, text and layout © Think Publishing 2006
The moral rights of the authors have been asserted

Editor: Joanna Eede
Designer: Lou Millward
Sub editor: Rica Dearman

ISBN-10 1-84525-013-3
ISBN-13 978-1-84525-013-3

Printed & bound in Singapore by KHL Printing Co.
The publishers and authors have made every effort to ensure the accuracy and currency of the information in *A Portrait of
England*. Similarly, every effort has been made to contact copyright holders. We apologise for any unintentional errors or
omissions. The publisher and authors disclaim any liability, loss, injury or damage incurred as a consequence, directly or
indirectly, of the use and application of the contents of this book.

Cover image: View from Scarth Wood Moor, above Swainsby on the North York Moors. Britainonview/Joe Cornish
All other photography credited on page 178.

The Campaign to Protect Rural England warmly thanks all those who have contributed words and photographs to this book. We dedicate it to the many thousands of volunteers who have worked so hard and given so freely of their time since we were founded in 1926.

Campaign to Protect
Rural England

FOREWORD

MAX HASTINGS
President, Campaign to Protect Rural England

MAX HASTINGS has lived in the English countryside for most of his life. A foreign correspondent in his younger days, he spent 16 years as editor of the London *Evening Standard* and editor-in-chief of *The Daily Telegraph*. He is the author of some 20 books, most on military history. He has been president of the CPRE since 2002.

This book is a celebration of the English countryside. We often speak about 'natural beauty', but in truth this is a misnomer. Although God does the best part, throughout its inhabited history the landscape has been shaped and managed by mankind.

The countryside has always changed, is changing and must continue to do so as the world moves on. Very many of the changes of the past 80 years – the years since the Campaign to Protect Rural England (CPRE) was founded in 1926 – have been destructive. But we should be inspired by how much there is left to fight for. Greatly as we may lament the mistakes and excesses of recent times, what is extraordinary is how much beauty survives. Anyone who knows the extraordinary diversity of the English countryside: its woods, hedges, lush river valleys, dramatic coastline, wild uplands and grassy downlands, knows that it is still one of the most beautiful in the world.

We hope this book will inspire all those who love the country, as well as give hope to those who suppose that its preservation is a lost cause. To paraphrase the old line about democracy, all that is needed for the English countryside to perish, amid the host of pressures which it now faces, is for good men and women to do nothing. For our landscape to survive, to succour and entrance our children and grandchildren, we must fight and keep fighting for its cause.

You have already helped, simply by buying this book. You might consider going a step further, by joining CPRE. Our purpose is not to demand that the countryside should be pickled in aspic, but rather that its precious qualities should be acknowledged in every decision that is made about is future: particularly concerning bulldozers and concrete.

Now relax, read on, and revel in the heady joys of rural England.

WINGPARK CLUMP,
BUCKINGHAMSHIRE

INTRODUCTION
JOANNA EEDE

It was always high on Bodmin Moor, not far past Jamaica Inn, that – according to my father – the tears would start. Not the tears of a dropped ice-cream, or the rough 'n' tumble tantrum of a back-seat fight with my brother, but the childish tears of separation from a landscape that had a profound impact from a young age: North Cornwall. The Moor was the border between imagination and reality, the point at which all that had captivated me – the clear light, the wailing gulls, the smell of gorse and salt, the roar and swell of the great moving Atlantic – gave way to the mundane and the motorway.

This anthology contains similar memories, opinions and beliefs expressed by diverse authors. All are testimony to why the Campaign to Protect Rural England has been working for nearly 80 years to preserve the English countryside. Even in our increasingly urban and materialistic world, it is clear from these contributions that rural England still inspires: by sailing the muddy creeks of Suffolk; by foraging for field mushrooms in the New Forest; by watching eel-fishers on the Dart; by witnessing a lamb being born or a sparrowhawk hovering.

The thoughts expressed draw on aesthetic appreciation of rural England; on the social history that has shaped its contours; on the atavistic pleasure in being part of nature's seasons and cycles; on the natural power of land and sea to enthrall and restore.

Importantly, the articles also highlight how many people are moved to protect the English countryside – from the worst effects of industrialised food production and consumer culture, from characterless dormitory developments, from a slow death due to thousands of unintended acts of thoughtlessness.

The contributions are as varied as the countryside itself. But several themes are evident: the English countryside is a spiritual antidote to the downsides of modern life, a wildlife haven to be conserved, a critical part of our ecological web. As Max Hastings says: 'We should be inspired by how much there is left to fight for.'

ILKLEY, WEST YORKSHIRE

CONTENTS

THE HUMAN CONNECTION 128

THE FUTURE 150

THE LIZARD, CORNWALL

WOODLAND, FLORA AND FUNGI

...As when, upon a tranced summer-night,
Those green-rob'd senators of mighty woods,
Tall oaks, branch-charmed by the earnest stars,
Dream, and so dream all night without a stir...

John Keats, 'Hyperion'

THE MEANING OF TREES

Alan Titchmarsh

I was asked recently to contribute to a television programme called *The Meaning of Life*. It's not that I understand it, but I reasoned that as nobody else did either I might as well chip in. Especially when they said that they would like to film me in a place close to my heart. I chose the small area of woodland that we planted above our old house about 14 years ago. That, I reasoned, while not in itself being 'the meaning of life', at least gave life some meaning, for me.

I've never been able to shake off the conviction that the only way to pay rent for one's time on Earth is to leave it in a better state than it was when one arrived. That might sound rather altruistic, and a touch simplistic, but it comes from the heart and is a pragmatic approach that I like to think I'm in the process of achieving.

Am I being smug? No. Just hopeful. The trees, when we planted them on the sloping field of Hampshire clay, were 6-in-high saplings. For the first four or five years, all we could see was a four-acre forest of green plastic tubes with large swathes of grass between them. These, I assured the family, were woodland rides. Well, 14 years on, they really are. We have oaks at 15 ft, wild cherry and ash at 20 ft and field maples and birches and beech trees, interplanted with holly and wayfaring tree, hawthorn and blackthorn.

To be able to take charge of a patch of land, and to help hand it back to nature is richly rewarding. Ah, you see, personal satisfaction comes into it as well; this was not a totally altruistic move after all. But to watch the deer browse among the undergrowth (now that the trees are safely out of reach and too thick to help with the fraying of their antlers), to see butterflies flitting across the glades of wildflowers, and to hear the alarmed call of a pheasant or the screech of an owl are ample recompense for the expense, and the work and the patience. And it salves my conscience, too. It helps me to believe that I've earned my keep.

Not everyone has the luxury of being able to plant a wood. But almost anyone can plant a native tree, and I hope everyone does – at least once in their life. They should plant it where they know it will be allowed to grow, and go and visit it on occasions, stroking their hand down its thickening trunk, watching its twigs swaying in the breeze, rejoicing when a bird makes its nest in its branches, for then it is properly a tree, and playing its own part in our potentially beautiful landscape.

It's a shame that the phrase 'tree-hugger' now has such a pejorative ring to it. I'm not a soul who believes that no tree should be felled. When they grow in the wrong place, or are well past their sell-by date, it is time to thank them for their efforts, make fires or furniture with their wood and replace them with new ones. But then I'll hug as many as you like.

TREE CANOPY,
SUSSEX

DECIDUOUS WOODLAND, SUSSEX

The wood I walk in on this mild May day, with the young yellow-brown foliage of the oaks between me and the blue sky, the white star-flowers and the blue-eyed speedwell and the ground ivy at my feet, what grove of tropic palms, what strange ferns or splendid broad-petalled blossoms, could ever thrill such deep and delicate fibres within me as this home scene? These familiar flowers, these well-remembered bird-notes, this sky, with its fitful brightness, these furrowed and grassy fields, each with a sort of personality given to it by the capricious hedgerows – such things as these are the mother-tongue of our imagination, the language that is laden with all the subtle, inextricable associations the fleeting hours of our childhood left behind them.

George Eliot, from *The Mill on the Floss*

HOW THE HARMLESS WANDERER IN THE WOODS BECAME A MORTAL ENEMY

George Monbiot

A few days ago, after a furious argument, I was thrown out of a wood where I have walked for over 20 years. I must admit that I did not behave very well. As I walked away I did something I haven't done for a long time: I gave the gamekeeper a one-fingered salute. In my defence I would plead that I was overcome with unhappiness and anger.

The time I have spent in that wood must amount to months. Every autumn I would spend days there, watching the turning colours or grubbing for mushrooms and beech mast and knapped flints. In the summer I would look for warblers and redstarts. I saw a nightjar there once. It was one of the few peaceful and beautiful places in my part of the world that's within a couple of miles of a station: I could escape from the traffic without a car. Part of me, I feel, belongs there. Or it did.

It is not that I wasn't trespassing before. Nor has the status of the land changed: it is still owned, as far as I know, by the same private estate. No one tried to stop me in those 20-odd years because no one was there. But now there is a blue plastic barrel every 50 yards, and the surrounding fields are planted with millet and maize. The wood has been turned into a pheasant run. Having scarcely figured in the landowner's books, it must now be making him a fortune. And I am perceived as a threat.

The words that rang in my ears as I stomped away were these: 'You've got your bloody right to roam now – why do you need to come here?' It struck me that this could be a perverse outcome of the legislation for which I spent years campaigning: that the right to walk in certain places is seen by landowners as consolidating their relations with the public. All that is not permitted will become forbidden.

But this, I expect, is a secondary problem. The more important one is surely the surge of money foaming through the southeast of England. A thousand woods can be filled with pheasants and still there are not enough to serve the people who have the money required – the many hundreds of pounds a day – to shoot them. We were told that the rising tide would lift all boats. But I feel I am drowning in it.

Two weeks ago, writing in the *Financial Times*, the economist Andrew Oswald observed that 'the hippies, the Greens, the road protesters, the downshifters, the slow-food movement – all are having their quiet revenge. Routinely derided, the ideas of these down-to-earth philosophers are being confirmed by new statistical work by psychologists and economists.' As I qualify on most counts, I will regard this as a vindication.

Oswald's point is that the industrialised countries have not become happier as they've become richer. Rates of depression and stress have risen, and people report no greater degree of satisfaction with their lives than their poorer ancestors did. In the United States, the sense of wellbeing has actually declined. One of the problems is that 'humans are creatures of comparison… it is relative income that matters: when everyone in a society gets wealthier, average wellbeing stays the same.'

The same point has been made recently by the New Economics Foundation and by Professor Richard Layard, in his book, *Happiness*. New developments in both psychological testing and neurobiology allow happiness to be measured with greater confidence than before. Layard cites research which suggests that it peaked in the United Kingdom in 1975. Beyond a certain degree of wealth – an average GDP of around $20,000 per head – 'additional income is not associated with extra happiness'.

Once a society's basic needs and comforts have been met, there is no point in becoming richer.

I am astonished by the astonishment with which their findings have been received. Compare, for example, these two statements:

'So one secret of happiness is to ignore comparisons with people who are more successful than you are: always compare downwards, not upwards.' Richard Layard, 2005.

'It put me to reflecting, how little repining there would be among mankind, at any condition of life, if people would rather compare their condition with those that are worse, in order to be thankful, than be always comparing them with those which are better, to assist their murmurings and complainings.' Daniel Defoe, 1719.

We have been led, by the thinking of people like the psychologist John B Watson and the economist Lionel Robbins, to forget what everyone once knew: that wealth and happiness are not the same thing.

Comparison is not the only reason the professors of happiness cite for our failure to feel better as we become richer. They point to the fact that we become habituated to wealth: Layard calls this 'the hedonic treadmill'. They blame the longer hours we work and our deteriorating relationships. But there is something I think they have missed: that wealth itself can become a source of deprivation.

Having money enhances your freedom. You can travel further and you can do more when you get there. But other people's money restricts your freedom. Where you once felt free, now you find fences. In fact, you *must* travel further to find somewhere in which you can be free.

As people become richer, and as they can extract more wealth from their property, other people become more threatening to them. We know that the fear of crime is a cause of unhappiness, but so is the sense of being seen as a potential criminal. The spikes and lights and cameras proclaim that society is not to be trusted, that we live in a world of Hobbesian relations. The story they tell becomes true, as property paranoia makes us hate each other. The harmless wanderer in the woods becomes a mortal enemy.

It is hard to see how that plague of pheasants could be deemed to have caused a net increase in happiness. A group of very wealthy people, who already have an endless choice of activities, have one more wood in which to shoot. The rest of us have one less wood in which to walk. The landowners tell us that by putting down birds they have an incentive to preserve the woods – this was one of the arguments the gamekeeper used as he was throwing me off. But what good does that do us if we are not allowed to walk there?

The Countryside and Rights of Way Act of 2000, which granted us the right to roam on mountains, moors, heath, downland and commons, has surely increased the sum of human happiness. But in those parts of the country which retain very little habitat of that kind (because it has been destroyed or enclosed by the landowners), the gains we made then might already have been cancelled out by the losses, as the landlords' new opportunities for making money reduce our opportunities for leaving money behind.

We need the full set of rights we were once promised, and which, in Scotland, have already been granted: access to the woods, the rivers and the coast as well as the open country. But as these places are turned into money-making monocultures, the question changes. Will we still want to visit them?

Out of this wood do not desire to go:
Thou shalt remain here, whether thou wilt or no.
I am a spirit of no common rate;
The summer still doth tend upon my state;
And I do love thee: therefore, go with me;
I'll give thee fairies to attend on thee,
And they shall fetch thee jewels from the deep,
And sing while thou on pressed flowers dost sleep;
And I will purge thy mortal grossness so
That thou shalt like an airy spirit go.
Peaseblossom! Cobweb! Moth! and Mustardseed!...

Be kind and courteous to this gentleman;
Hop in his walks and gambol in his eyes;
Feed him with apricocks and dewberries,
With purple grapes, green figs, and mulberries;
The honey-bags steal from the humble-bees,
And for night-tapers crop their waxen thighs
And light them at the fiery glow-worm's eyes,
To have my love to bed and to arise;
And pluck the wings from painted butterflies
To fan the moonbeams from his sleeping eyes:
Nod to him, elves, and do him courtesies.

William Shakespeare, Titania's speech from
A Midsummer Night's Dream

ASH SEEDLING

BLESSED BY OAKS

Adam Nicolson

The whole of our farm, on a poor bit of land in the Sussex Weald, should be wood really. Wood is what grows best here and we're blessed with trees. One of our neighbours, a young dairy farmer called Stephen Wrenn, who took our grazing for his bullocks one summer, said to me as we were having a drink together: 'I don't know a farm that's as lucky as this one with its trees. You'll look after your oaks, won't you?'

Stephen was killed six months later, when a tractor he was driving toppled over a little bank, no higher than the back of a chair, as his father described it to me, and crushed his head.

He'd come back that day from his honeymoon and the entire village was in shock over his death. Two or three hundred people went to the funeral and the vicar, who a couple of weeks previously had married him, helped bury him, too.

Stephen and I had long talks the previous summer about what to do with this land. He was all for giving up the dairy herd and turning the family farm, Perryman's, just over the hill from us, to the new short rotation willow coppice which can be harvested every couple of years and burnt for energy. So that last spring they sold their cows and Brian, Stephen's father, went on to sell his milk quota. But it was such a dry year with so little thick growth in the grass – all top and no bottom, as they say here – that no one was in the market to take on extra capacity, since feeding the cattle the following winter would cost a fortune in hay.

So the Wrenns, Stephen's young widow and his parents, all still together at Perryman's, sat tight, marking time, trying to accommodate this thing that had happened. You could see one of their very banky fields across the little valley at the edge of our land. The year before it had been grazed tight, thistly and docky in patches like every bit of land round here, but with a background of new, bright green grass.

That year, with the cows gone, and then with Stephen gone, it looked different, the hay long and not cut until late, an air of abandonment to it, or at least of other matters on the mind. I looked across at that field and in it saw what had happened to the Wrenn family, the stupid, trivial, devastating disaster, the slice taken out of their lives.

Still now, 12 years later, I remember Stephen for the grinning optimism of what he said about the trees, the way we were lucky, blessed with the oaks here. Isn't it a habit in some part of the world to plant a tree on a person's grave, to fertilise a cherry or an apple of one's own? It seems like a good idea. That, anyway, is the picture I now have of Stephen Wrenn. But it is an oak not a fruit tree that is springing from his grave, the big-limbed, dark green, thick-boled, spreading, ancient kind of oak, so solid a part of the country here that it is known as the Sussex Weed.

There is something not right, though, about that picture. It is no more than a heraldic image of the tree, clarified and simplified. If you actually look closely at an oak, it is not really the perfect, enlarged cauliflower floret you see on pub signs or in the sanitised imagination. And no year, oddly enough, revealed that, to me anyway, more starkly than the one following Stephen died. Perhaps I hadn't really looked before, but that year, for months, the trees looked bruised and battered.

A ride on the Northern Line in the evening rush hour would not reveal a more exhausted line of faces than the trees long displayed. Even at the end of July, their leaves already looked used, dirty and in need of replacement. By early August, some of the hawthorn and hornbeams in the hedges were already largely yellow. And by the end of the month, the spindle leaves were spotted black and had dried at the edges into a pair of narrow red curling lips. Elders had gone bald before their time and there were ash trees of which whole sections had been a dead manila brown for weeks.

It was, of course, the heat, or more perhaps the drought. An oak tree drinks for England. It is a huge and silent pump, a humidifier of the air, drawing mineral sustenance from the daily lakes of water that pass through it. Where in a summer like that could such a tree have got the income it needed?

The truth was, at least with some of the oaks here, they had been running on empty, trying to live through a grinding climatic recession. And as with any big organisation, in the face of difficulty, spontaneous damage seemed to occur all too easily.

I was fencing between Cottage and Target fields – the sheep had, as ever, been getting through – and I leant on a low oak branch as I unwound the wire. As I pushed against it, quite unconsciously, without any real effort, the branch, perhaps 15 or 20 ft long, came away from the trunk of the tree and dropped slowly to the ground. It had seemed fully alive, decked with leaves and new acorns as much as any other, but it pulled away as softly and as willingly as the wing-bone of a well-cooked chicken. I pushed it into the fence, as an extra sheep deterrent.

Two days later, at the top of the Slip field, I found an enormous branch, lying full of leaves and acorns, on the ground beneath its parent, perhaps 40 ft long, the bulk of a small house or a lorry. It, too, had been neatly severed at the base, as if the branch had been sacked, ruthlessly dropped for the greater good of the whole.

These living branches rejected in mid-season made me look at the oak tree in a new light: their scarred bodies, the withered limbs, the usual asymmetry to their outlines, the slightly uneven track taken by each branch as it moves out from the main stem. And the new way of seeing the oak was this: not as a thing whole and neatly inevitable in itself, but as the record of its own history of survival and failure, retraction and extension, stress and abundance. Each oak has a visible history and the story it tells is more like the history of a human family, forever negotiating hazards, accommodating loss, reshaping its existence, as Brian Wrenn said to me one evening as we sat looking at the sea near Rye Harbour, to face a different future.

They shut the road through the woods
Seventy years ago.
Weather and rain have undone it again,
And now you would never know
There was once a road through the woods
Before they planted the trees.
It is underneath the coppice and heath,
And the thin anemones.
Only the keeper sees
That, where the ring-dove broods,
And the badgers roll at ease,
There was once a road through the woods.

Yet, if you enter the woods
Of a summer evening late,
When the night-air cools on the trout-ringed pools
Where the otter whistles his mate.
(They fear not men in the woods,
Because they see so few)
You will hear the beat of a horse's feet,
And the swish of a skirt in the dew,
Steadily cantering through
The misty solitudes,
As though they perfectly knew
The old lost road through the woods...
But there is no road through the woods.

Rudyard Kipling, 'The Way Through the Woods'

WOODLAND ADVENTURING

Sir Ranulph Fiennes

There is a field in West Sussex between the hamlet of River and the village of Lodsworth which I loved as a child. It is bound by woodland, and its eastern rim is cut by the river Lod; a small bridge, from which people would fish for eel, crosses the water. Then, there were tadpoles and frogs in every puddle, and the old woods on the other side of the bridge were alive with butterflies by day and glow-worms and owls by night. In the long school holidays my friends and I roamed the woods, camped in the trees and built dugouts in the earthy cliff sides. It was an adventuring paradise for teenagers.

DARK GREEN FRITILLARY
FEEDING ON BRAMBLE

*We're on the way to the wood, where our tyres slide
again on the soft and squashy mattress of fallen leaves.
The sun is shining through the beech trees which stand,
like pillars in the sea, deep in the haze of bluebells. The
food and bottles, which have come in big baskets built
to be slung on the backs of Moroccan donkeys, are
unloaded. The dogs are jumping over the bluebells and
the children are running down the hill after them. My
chair, ridiculously solid, has also been carried from the car
and I'm sitting on it like some absurd Canute making a
drawing room of the wood and giving orders to the
advancing tide of wild flowers. I feel neither old nor in
any way incapacitated. Everything is perfectly all right.*

Sir John Mortimer, from *The Summer of a
Dormouse: A Year of Growing Old Disgracefully*

BLUEBELL WOOD, SUSSEX

NEW FOREST FUNGUS

Jonathan Meades

There never was a time when I didn't search for fungi. From earliest childhood I would be woken in the dark and piled breakfastless into my father's rickety car. Dawn would barely be breaking when we crossed the vaporous floated meadows of the Ebble and began the wheezing ascent to the downs where certain fields – 'our fields' – would be constellated white like a driving range. An hour or so later we would return home to the edge of Salisbury, baskets brimming, appetite whetted, to a breakfast of field mushrooms and horse mushrooms, bacon, eggs.

Of my father's hunter-gatherer pursuits this is the only one I enjoyed: beating pheasants was boring; shivering beside March leets whilst he fished for the first run of salmon was boring and cold. And my enjoyment of mushrooming was far from entire. It was mitigated by the chalky open terrain where, save mushrooms, there grew only grass, thistles, blackthorns and rusting water butts. The pleasure was in the gathering. Not in the landscape. In Welsh and French *cwm* and *combe* signify a valley. In Wiltshire-English coomb signifies a riverless valley. Such valleys frightened me: I identified one, in particular, as the 'Valley of the Shadow of Death' (clunkily renamed 'the darkest valley', which doesn't do the trick).

The terrain that delighted me began, however, only a few miles away. Grassless, coombless, sylvan and – when I was a child – fungusless. I don't mean that the New Forest was bereft of fungi but, despite my mother having gathered 'penny buns' there when she was a child, I was brought up in ignorance of the esculent properties of 'toadstools'. That typically English ignorance, born of mycophobia, was

COMMON PUFFBALL,
NEW FOREST

eventually allayed in my teens by the tenant peasant at a friend's château in Entre Deux Mers. He obligingly taught me to identify the few species worth gathering and the few that are harmful: most are neither gastronomically interesting nor poisonous. There is, unsurprisingly, no English word for the slangy *cepeux*. It means abounding in ceps. The New Forest does just that.

This new knowledge reinvigorated My Forest, granted my childhood playground a change of use suitable to adolescence and adulthood. Searching for fungus is the very opposite of playing golf. It is a Good Walk improved. It is the greatest of autumnal pleasures. And if you gather nothing, well so be it – for you will have leaf-peeped and spotted jays and smelled woodsmoke and touched velvet moss and pondered the source of droppings. Are these spraints or are they fewmets? The latter is more likely, for they are the faecal matter of deer which are everywhere.

A few Octobers ago in a thicket at Bramshaw I came face to face with a magnificently, baroquely bez-tined stag with the build of a bull. It was, thankfully, more alarmed than I was – it bolted. But otters? They certainly live within the confines of the Otter, Owl and Wildlife Park. It is characteristic of the new New Forest that there should be signs warning drivers that these cuddly lovable creatures may be crossing the road: proclaiming their presence. (Vipers have yet to enjoy kindred advertisements.)

Parts of the old New Forest constituted an illusory wilderness, the best that suburbanised southern England could manage. Now, that illusion has not been entirely ruptured, but it is certainly more fragile than it once was.

FROM THE RIVER TO THE SEA

By a high star our course is set, our end is Life. Put out to sea.

Louis MacNeice, 'Thalassa'

The sea runs back against itself
With scarcely time for breaking wave
To cannonade a slatey shelf
And thunder under in a cave.

Before the next can fully burst
The headwind, blowing harder still,
Smooths it to what it was at first –
A slowly rolling water-hill.

Against the breeze the breakers haste,
Against the tide their ridges run
And all the sea's a dappled waste
Criss-crossing underneath the sun.

Far down the beach the ripples drag
Blown backward, rearing from the shore,
And wailing gull and shrieking shag
Alone can pierce the ocean roar.

Unheard, a mongrel hound gives tongue,
Unheard are shouts of little boys;
What chance has any inland lung
Against this multi-water noise?

Here where the cliffs alone prevail
I stand exultant, neutral, free,
And from the cushion of the gale
Behold a huge consoling sea.

John Betjeman, 'Winter Seascape'

BEDRUTHAN STEPS, CORNWALL

THE SUFFOLK COAST

Ralph Fiennes

I was born in Suffolk and spent the first six years of my life growing up just outside Southwold. Although thought of as 'flat', the Suffolk landscape is full of unusual undulations, small mysterious roads that make a beguiling network through land that changes with unusual subtlety. The coast and marshes near Walberswick and Dunwich are well known, but I have strong childhood associations with the beaches there. I remember playing on Southwold beach thinking I would try to dig through the sand to Australia. The North Sea carries an ominous power – its grey green waves swollen by Arctic winds. The East Anglian skies are massive and their vastness is overwhelming and uplifting. The Suffolk horizon line, often broken by the silhouettes of churches and woodland, contrasts the ordered farm land with the unremitting presence of the sky.

DUNWICH

ALDEBURGH, SUFFOLK

DRURIDGE BAY, NORTHUMBERLAND

THE MEANING OF MUD

Libby Purves

To the sailor and the dreamer alike, the great rock harbours of the West have obvious romance: Drake in his hammock, slung a'tween the round shot in Nombre Dios Bay, is dreaming of Plymouth Hoe. The Old Sea Rat in *The Wind in the Willows* longs for the blue and grey notch of Fowey; Salcombe and Falmouth throw rocky arms around the mariner now as they have done since Viking days.

But here in the East, it is different: tricky, sly, muddy, changeable. Along the south coast several of the Cinque Ports of Elizabethan times and ceremonial fame are not even ports any more: just bland silty beaches with no shelter, or perhaps an apologetic trickle of a creek dribbling to the sea. Others, like Rye, are harbours still, but fit only for locals and the brave. Eastbourne has had to build itself an artificial marina, with a long, difficult dredged channel to follow, and to avoid like the plague in an onshore wind.

Sail round the corner, past the Downs where fleets have sheltered from westerly gales since fleets began, and you find tatty, friendly Ramsgate and mercantile Harwich, separated by the nightmare grey labyrinth of the Thames Estuary and approached by winding through more sandbanks. The sailor follows buoys often barely visible against the sluicing tidal murk. Then the rivers of Deben and Ore, Lowestoft with another awkward approach, and the few and treacherous harbours of North Norfolk and the Wash. And before you come to the certainties of granite and limestone again, you must pass – or attempt to enter – Bridlington and Whitby with their gallant breakwaters and long, long piers; piers

between which, at low water, police horses can trot for their daily exercise.

Yet the East coast harbours and creeks have their own fascination. Mud is a medium, too, a habitat and a challenge. Glance from the train at Manningtree one day and you see nothing but water, bland and innocent, with little yachts bobbing at anchor. Next time, at a different tide, you glance through the same window and there is a world of shining pockmarked mud haunted by a thousand wading birds. Boats lie slumped here and there on the ooze, and only a thread of deeper water winds through it all, demonstrating why those buoys must be followed faithfully if the sailor is ever to escape.

Or find your way, cautiously, up the river Ore until it becomes the Alde at Aldeburgh, and persist, in as small and shallow a boat as you can find, in wriggling upriver on a rising tide. No more buoys here: just withies, sticks, bearing either tatters of green cloth or old red paint tins. Take a sharp dog-leg turn under Iken church and you are among the reeds, heading inland to Snape Maltings. Rivers like this are half threat, half promise; on the one hand you might sail downstream and out to sea and find a whole world, where the water glows green and blue instead of brown, and nothing can stop you from sailing on to Rio or the Cape. On the other hand rivers are brown sneaks, probing into the safe lush countryside. Invaders might creep up them and stake a claim, as vikings crept up the Deben to Sutton Hoo. I once wrote a novel, *Regatta*, in which the Alde and Ore was the main character, so strong a hold does this stretch of water take on the imagination.

AN ESSEX ESTUARY

But of all the East coast harbour sights – mud, curlews, herons, the occasional resting seal – the one I find which stirs me most is man-made. There is something immensely moving about a breakwater: along this changeable, eroding sandy coastline the great walls thrown out into the North Sea – the best of them far to the North, in Yorkshire and Humberside – seem like the ultimate human defiance of fate and mortality. They are symbols of determination to set forth on unfriendly waters, and tokens of faith in a safe return. Nature did not make this coast safe, or hospitable, or predictable. Man has, with cautious respect, at least tried to. But Man also knows that it can't last. Where I live, at Dunwich, there was a great port in the fourteenth century. Now there is a muddy creek, a few houses and a great bird-haunted emptiness. *Tout lasse, tout passe, tout casse*. Perhaps it is because the East knows this, and is humble, that it holds such fascination.

Leaving the main stream, they now passed into what seemed at first sight like a little land-locked lake. Green turf sloped down to either edge, brown snaky tree-roots gleamed below the surface of the quiet water, while ahead of them the silvery shoulder and foamy tumble of a weir, arm-in-arm with a restless dripping mill-wheel, that held up in its turn a grey-gabled mill-house, filled the air with a soothing murmur of sound, dull and smothery, yet with little clear voices speaking up cheerfully out of it at intervals. It was so very beautiful that the Mole could only hold up both forepaws and gasp, 'O my! O my! O my!'

Kenneth Grahame, from *The Wind in the Willows*

BUDLEIGH SALTERTON, DEVON

THE RIVER ARUN, SUSSEX

WILD, WILD DODMAN
Tim Smit

The magic of the Dodman is that it is so unforgiving. Raw, wind-blasted. Lichen-crusted granite noses into the sea and plunges sheer to the ocean floor. These rocks are rounded, female, and here and there soft depressions in the sea of bracken betray an old mine and even a pair of big divots where a Junker 88 dropped its load in 1942, lost in the clouds and miles off course for Falmouth. Occasionally the National Trust has shaved the bracken to nurture patchwork pastures for 'Thelwell'-looking hill ponies.

Viewed from the sea the sense of menace is real. The water is black and a rip current broils and tumbles at all times save slack water.

Why do I love it so? This place is where the only trees, black and whitethorn, grow in stunted stoop, a witch's salute, a bending rictus in homage to the ever-present wind. Look closely and you see a different side. For unforgiving rock read fortress. For sunken lane read ditch and rampart. This was an Iron Age hill fort. Impregnable, and its flat pastures contained within the ramparts play tricks with the imagination. You can imagine the huts, the enclosed flocks, the smithy working and the hubbub of a people not so different to us.

For me, the real magic is the walk along the ditch on the leeward side on the roughest day you could light a match here. To one side field walls and hedgerows, to the other a rampart now covered in wildflowers that towers above you. It runs east to west and in spring this is a quarter of a mile of pure paradise. Such a profusion that I've never seen anywhere else: foxgloves, herb Robert, pink campion, celandine, Alexander, primroses, cow parsley, drifts of valerian and my own favourite, the delicate toadflax. It is here, in the shadow of the rampart that I feel the gentle melancholy that passes for real happiness. Bittersweet maybe, but the sense of abundance and the softness underfoot, the hum of insects and the lush, lush grass, broken only by the paths of the creatures that have made this place home is deeply satisfying. It is timeless, but also, now.

It sounds funny, but there have been evenings when I have walked here alone, when I have felt the air heavy on me as if it were the fug of company and raised the hair on the back of my neck. It was not sinister, it felt companionable. By what, I do not know, maybe nature itself.

DODMAN POINT,
CORNWALL

NEAR CRASTER

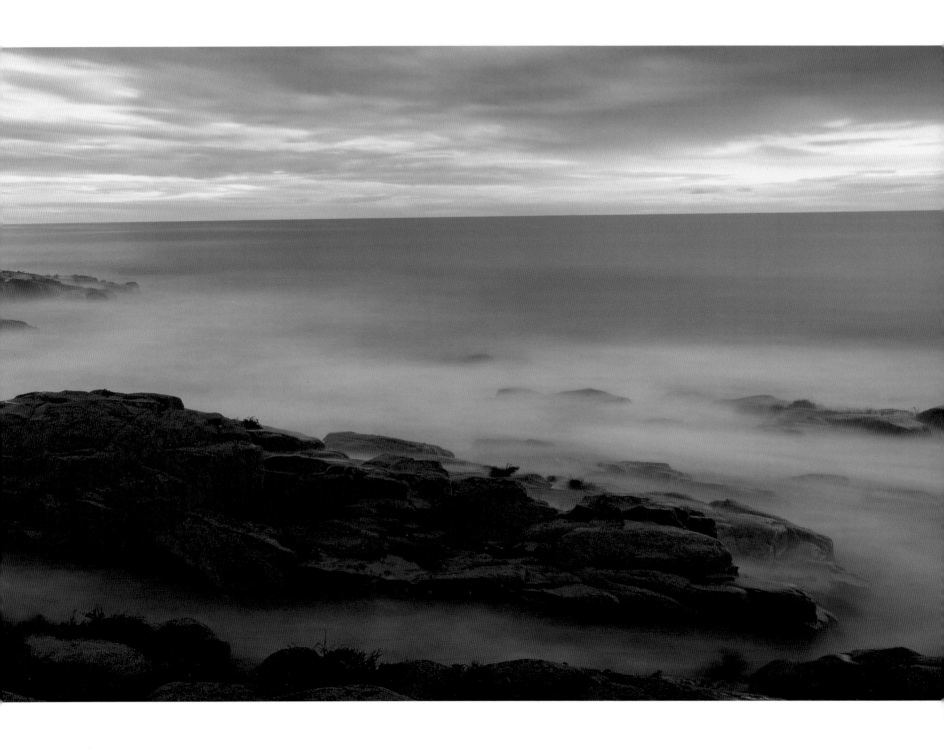

FROM THE RIVER TO THE SEA

...(two places I've seen eels, bright whips of flow
like stopper waves the rivercurve slides through
trampling around at first you just make out
the elver movement of the running sunlight
three foot under the road-judder you hold
and breathe contracted to an eye-quiet world
while an old dandelion unpicks her shawl
and one by one the small spent oak flowers fall
then gently lift a branch brown tag and fur
on every stone and straw and drifting burr
when like a streamer from your own eye's iris
a kingfisher spurts through the bridge whose axis
is endlessly in motion as each wave
photos its flowing to the bridge's curve
if you can keep your foothold, snooping down
then suddenly two eels let go get thrown
tumbling away downstream looping and linking
another time we scooped a net through sinking
silt and gold and caught one strong as bike-chain
stared for a while then let it back again
I never pass that place and not make time
to see if there's an eel come up the stream
I let time go as slow as moss, I stand
and try to get the dragonflies to land
their gypsy-coloured engines on my hand)

Alice Oswald, from 'Dart'

RIVER DART

OF TIME
AND HISTORY

Time present and time past
Are both perhaps present in time future,
And time future contained in time past.

TS Eliot, 'Four Quartets'

ROOTED IN LANDSCAPE

Dr Richard Muir

POLLARDED ASH

All my life, I have been involved with historic countryside: mesmerised by its beauty, tantalised by its complexities and tormented by its destruction. As time has passed, it has taught me certain truths, and these have gained in strength as experience has mounted. I lost one of my first commissions as a writer when I refused to describe how country people had 'deliberately' created beautiful scenery. I knew all too well that the landscapes that inspire and sustain us today were workaday countrysides. Their grandeur was a by-product of a struggle for survival by people who lived with oppression and famine; who watched helplessly as their babies died, and who generally died quite young, with infected teeth and arthritis-ridden bodies. Certainly, the wonderful settings that they and their forbears had created must have given them solace and wonderment, but one could not gnaw on a view.

Next, I began to appreciate, more and more, that there is an explanation for every little facet of a scene. Each stump, track, stone scatter and ditch has its reason and story. However, gaining a true appreciation of an historic landscape is a mighty challenge. Those who attempt to gain one in a hurry, with vacuous computer programmes, reveal only the shallowness of their understanding. As a student, I thought that geomorphology, the study of physical landforms, offered the supreme intellectual challenge, but then I saw that the human element in landscape creation provided an extra element of perversity. The fascination has never waned, and even when the obliteration of much-loved scenes has brought me to despair I can still attempt to detach myself and see a landscape as a great crossword puzzle spanning the horizons, one with clues, red herrings, blind alleys and revelations.

Also, I came to realise that each society creates countryside in its own image. If we are bland, materialistic and cowardly there can be no hiding all this, for our mark will be there, scarring the hills and vales, for those who follow to see. It is not simply a case or good and bad, for the harsh Tudor landlords who tore down villages and turned their fields into sheep runs left a charming legacy of hedged pastures in their place. In any journey across Britain, the rambler will experience the mass mysticism that created the great tombs and temples of the late Neolithic period and the soaring spires and towers of medieval Christianity. These were times when the spiritual passions brewing in minds and hearts erupted and spilled out across the landscape. Will our golf ranges, time-share chalets and theme parks have quite the same allure? (My favourite modern legacy lies on the fringe of my native village, where a housing estate is tastefully named after the last surviving fragment of a medieval wood – one that was felled to allow its construction.)

All the while, gradually accumulating evidence has conveyed the message that in historic countrysides, things need not be what they seem to be or what the books claim them to be. I will attempt to demonstrate this by considering ancient trees, a topic that has fascinated me for the last decade. In parts of Nidderdale, twisted oak trees that are several hundreds of years old are dotted around, forming eye-catchers within the fieldscape. The most unreliable explanation is the one provided by local people, who will tell you that the trees are the last relics of the medieval Forest of Knaresborough. In fact, like most royal forests, Knaresborough embraced a wide spectrum of land uses, of which woodland was just one. A close inspection of old maps and earthworks on the ground show that the surviving trees form alignments and are linked

by faint ridges or ridges and troughs. These are the traces of hedgerows and ditches, for our ancient oaks were never woodland trees and almost all originated in hedgerows. As mounting curiosity took me to the old documents, I discovered when these hedgerow trees were planted, for the dismantling of the common fields in Tudor and Elizabethan times resulted in the establishment of miles and miles of tree-studded hedgerows to mark out the new fields.

All the trees have been beheaded or pollarded. Pollards were the trees of the common people. From their crowns, above the reach of browsing, sprang the crops of poles used for fuel and the leafy loppings used as browse. The medieval leases issued by Fountains Abbey show that pollarding had a long tradition, with tenants being allowed to lop 'greenhews' or 'water boughs' for their stock or the deer, but being forbidden to fell trees. (Their tenants also leased 'hollins' or holly groves, from which thornless leaves cut from the tops of the trees were stored as winter fodder.) This then led me to a closer perusal of medieval illustrations – in which virtually every tree represented can be recognised as a pollard. Also, I looked at the landscape parks in the region, and saw that the twisted pollards studding their lawns had not been planted and positioned by famous landscapers. Instead, they were hedgerow trees engulfed and lassoed by the boundaries of new parks and redeployed in scenic roles. The final irony is that the grotesquely contorted pollards seen in today's fieldscapes are a testimony to the modern neglect of rural traditions. The medieval trees were re-pollarded every dozen years or so. Ours have grown unchecked since pollarding was abandoned a couple of centuries or more ago. So now, the boughs grow ever thicker and heavier, until, one by one, they snap away from their hollowed trunk. All this is one of just

many examples of how the historic features of our countrysides reward enquiry with surprises and vastly enhanced understanding.

Finally, it must be said that landscapes offer mental balm as well as intellectual stimulation. The creators of historic countryside were steeped in their settings, being as much parts of them as the trees, ploughland and pond life. Changing lifestyles have made us footloose, and with this, has come insecurity. Being uncertain about the settings that shaped us, we are uncertain about our very selves. Weary of change and travel, we may land in one place and seek, desperately, to fabricate an identity. An enhanced awareness of that setting gives us an opportunity to become rooted in it, and the more intensely we discover the nuances of place and its story, the more rooted we may become. (Swelling, meanwhile, may be the readiness to defend that place from the worst aspects of modernity that threaten both it and ourselves.) Eventually, one may reach a state or realising that where we are is an important part of what we are. I believe that a fascination with historic landscape can help to reach this state.

CASTLERIGG STONE CIRCLE, CUMBRIA

WALKING THROUGH HISTORY
Penelope Lively

I have a lifelong commitment to Somerset; specifically, that area within the angle of Exmoor and the Brendons, from Minehead and Watchet on the coast inland to a cluster of villages – Washford, Withycombe, Roadwater, Luxborough, the little market town of Williton. Tipping hills, deep lanes, reddish-pink earth, the pewter line of the sea, fringed by the distant Welsh coast, the long slack contours of the moor. My family roots are here; we have a toehold still. I've known the place since I was six, and nothing has changed: the same hedge is good for blackberries, a buzzard wheels above the Comberow valley, you can find ammonites on Blue Anchor beach.

Except, of course, that there has been plenty of change. The branch line to Minehead on which I travelled when I was a schoolgirl is now a scenic railway, doing good business. There are brown signs everywhere; the area is into serious tourism now, of necessity. There are facilities undreamed of in the 1950s: pubs that serve food – good food at that; supermarkets – a Sainsbury's delivery van gamely picking its way through the lanes. People are living differently; there are more of them, especially in summer when half the population seems to tip into the West Country. But the bones of the place are the same; in our little corner, barely a field boundary has altered, there is little new building – Exmoor National Park covers much of the area, with its draconian planning regulations. And in August, when the coast is teeming, and the car parks up on the moor are glittering, you can walk up Croydon Hill and never meet a soul, and indeed the same would be true of most of the footpaths and bridleways.

English landscape reflects what has happened here, from Iron Age hillforts to ridge and furrow and the hedge lines of parliamentary enclosure. Maybe in centuries to come the archaeological remains of the swooping white tent structure of Butlins at Minehead will be scrutinised for revelations about leisure activities in a bygone era. Change is inevitable; countryside is not just scenery, but a workspace, and the way in which it is worked alters from century to century. To understand something of landscape history is to be able to read the place, as well as see it – to understand why that track goes the way it does, what those lumps and bumps in a field suggest. A track still known locally as the mineral line runs from the Brendon hills down to Watchet harbour. This is the ghost of the railway incline that once took iron ore down from the workings on the hill for shipment over the steelworks in Wales. Up on the moor, there is shadow of a ninth-century long-distance route – the Harepath, followed by Saxon farmers when called for military

EXMOOR

service. In the woodland of the Luxborough valley there is a place called the Druid's Grave – a Bronze Age burial site, in fact. Everywhere, there are these hints of what has gone on here – a hundred years ago, a thousand years ago.

A perfect west Somerset day, for me, would include a walk up Horner Water, one of the most exquisite of the combes that plunge down from the moor, fish and chips on the esplanade at Watchet, after a potter along Blue Anchor beach, looking for ammonites and picking up chunks of pink and grey alabaster that falls from the seams in the cliffs behind. Then maybe a spot of church visiting: Old Cleeve, with its lovely churchyard looking out towards the hills and the sea – my grandparents are buried there, and my aunty; St Bartholomew's, Rodhuish – a beautifully simple twelfth-century chapel, with one of the few surviving musicians' galleries. It is going to be a long day, and I'd want also to climb down Bossington Point for the view along the coast and over Porlock Vale. Oh, and there would

have to be a stop at Cleeve Abbey, the Cistercian monastery at Washford that is an English Heritage site now, carefully restored, but that in my schooldays was an unassuming ruin, open on Wednesday afternoons only, supervised by a lady called Miss Cleeva Clapp, who had been born nearby and named after the abbey.

I am not fussy as to season, so far as this perfect day goes. In winter, there would be the scoured red fields, the skeletal shape of trees. By spring, the hedge-banks would be cliffs of primroses, there would be a green mist over the fields, the warblers would have arrived. Summer would mean swallows and sometimes a lark (nothing like as many as there used to be), village fêtes and long, light evenings. Autumn would give me scarlet berries and flocks of finches spraying up from the stubble. Thanks heaven for the English climate and the seasonal variety that makes a familiar landscape change its skin month by month.

LIMESTONE PAVEMENTS, MALHAM

Buried in time and sleep,
So drowsy, so overgrown,
That here the moss is green upon the stone,
And lichen stains the keep.

Vita Sackville-West, from 'Sissinghurst'

THE VILLAGE BLACKSMITH

Roy Hattersley

East Bergholt is just off the A12 midway between Ipswich and Colchester and so near to both of those boroughs that only a miracle can have saved it from being swamped by urban sprawl. But East Bergholt is not a suburb. It is still a village and one of the few places in all of England where a blacksmith still bends and breaks hot metal on an old-fashioned anvil. Rodney Moss works in much the same way as his father and grandfather did before him. But the Moss family was regarded in Victorian East Bergholt as newcomers to the trade. The forge, in which it has now worked for three generations, first shod horses in the fifteenth century. Experts have dated the original parts of the building to some time between 1450 and 1500 – as Rodney Moss puts it: 'Before Henry VIII started chopping off people's heads'.

Horseshoes are made and fitted there no more. During the years when tractors began to take over from Suffolk Punches and Clydesdales in the fields, but recreational riding had not become a weekend pastime, Rodney Moss and his father turned their attention to the other half of their trade – gates, railings and anything else that could be made from metal. These days, modern farriers travel the country and shoe horses in riding schools and livery stables. Rodney Moss, being a traditional craftsman, waits in his place of business for customers to come to him. The trophies of the old trade still hang on the forge walls. The Moss family, being masters of their craft, made every sort of horseshoe. Some were designed to clip onto hooves rather than be nailed. Others were serrated on the side that hits the ground so as to provide a better grip in icy weather. The shoes share hooks, opposite the furnace, with massive iron bits (which must have been forged for huge shire horses with mighty jaws) and ancient iron harness

buckles. They have hung there since the days when a boy pumped away with bellows to make the coal and coke burn bright. Now, at the flick of a switch, an electric fan does the job in seconds.

Despite the benefits of modern living, Rodney Moss 'misses shoeing terribly'. By mastering new methods and materials he has maintained a thriving business. But he is unapologetically nostalgic for the years when: 'Farm workers would come in with repairs, sit down on the boxes alongside the walls, eat their midday meals – thick wedges of cheese and raw onions – and talk about the days when they were lads. In the old days, we went into the fields at harvest time to help, to watch and to glean' – gleaning being the collection of the wheat and barley that the mowing machine had missed. 'We used to chase the rabbits with sticks. And sometimes we caught them and took them home for supper.' Rodney Moss, though barely of retirement age, talks of the rural idyll which is the vision of old England – the arcadia which John Constable once painted.

Flatford Mill – once the home of the Constable family – is barely a mile away from Rodney Moss's forge. The water wheel no longer turns and reeds grow in the lock. It is now a fieldwork centre which offers courses that aim to bring 'environmental understanding' to students who range from GCSE candidates to holidaymakers enjoying what the brochure calls 'leisure learning'. Both the mill and Willie Lott's house (which the centre also owns) are instantly recognisable from Constable's paintings – paintings to which the forge can claim to have made a distinct contribution. The haywain – the subject of Constable's most famous landscape – was almost certainly pulled by horses which had been shod there. What is more, the iron tyres on the haywain's wheels were probably

made under the same timbered roof. In Constable's day there was a wheelwright's workshop next door. And we know that he, and the Moss family's predecessors, worked in partnership. The ancient beam-drill, which bored nail holes into the cold iron, can still be swung out across the forge floor.

When next you visit the National Gallery or see a print of *The Haywain*, remember that (as well as a work of genius) it is a memorial to England's traditional trades. These days, the forge concentrates on work which its uninitiated customers still call 'wrought iron' even though it is made from mild steel. Rodney Moss no longer needs to heat his strips of metal up to a temperature at which, almost at melting point, they fuse into each other to create the joints and joins in gates and railings. The parts and pieces are spot-welded together. But the old craftsmanship remains. Rodney Moss can still take a piece of steel and, by the skill of his hand and judgement of his eye, turn it into a perfectly symmetrical spiral. At East Bergholt, old and modern England meet in a forge which has stood on the same spot for more than five hundred years.

JESSOP'S JAUNT
David Foster

A narrow lane leads over Chisbury hill fort and winds down into the village of Great Bedwyn. Great where? Precisely. On a cold winter's morning, with a sharp frost pricking my face and a thick white mist draining the colour from the landscape, it felt as if I'd arrived at the end of the Earth.

In fact, this thriving community of red-brick houses and colour-washed cottages lies on the outskirts of Savernake Forest, just a few miles south of the Marlborough Downs. Beyond the tight rollercoaster of hump-backed bridges that links the village to the nearby Kennet and Avon canal, I stamped about on the wharf in the forlorn hope of coaxing some blood back into my frozen limbs.

It was tempting to start walking here, pounding the canal towpath as it slips westwards through Bedwyn's backyards. But, instead, I wanted to see one of the most eccentric collections in Britain, tucked away in the heart of the village. Not for the faint-hearted, Lloyd's stone museum is a flamboyant extravaganza; a charming village house almost entirely submerged beneath a complete kit of parts for a decent-sized Victorian cemetery.

John Lloyd, whose family has run the village stonemason's for seven generations, explains how his ancestors settled here after helping to build the canal at the end of the eighteenth century. The collection came later, he told me, starting with two big plaster friezes that came back from the Great Exhibition of 1851. The firm had no use for them, says John, so they put them on the side of the house. As you do.

John's grandfather added a couple of apprentice pieces. Years later, his father, Benjamin, put most of the memorials on the front wall, along with anything else that was 'a bit too interesting or novel'. John points across the yard to a 3-ft-high confection near the gate. 'I put the pineapple up, just on the corner there,' he says carelessly, much as you or I might nip out and plant a few bulbs.

Leaving the village through the swirling mists of St Mary's churchyard, I rejoined the canal at Bedwyn Church Lock. The stillness was absolute, broken only by the deep, rhythmic *woomph… woomph…* of water surging and bubbling into the lock chamber like gases from a volcanic spring. A couple of dog walkers loomed out of the mist but, for the most part, I passed unnoticed up the locks towards Crofton Pumping Station.

If engineer John Rennie had got his way, the canal would have plunged into a long tunnel at Crofton. For two-and-a-half laborious miles, boatmen would have manhandled their craft through the darkness whilst their horses frolicked in the fresh air on the towpath above their heads. But the directors baulked at such an expensive project, opting instead for William Jessop's proposal to carry the canal over the low hill at Burbage.

The problem, explained Ray Knowles, chairman of the canal trust's Crofton branch, as he thrust a restorative mug of hot chocolate into my hand, was that Jessop's scheme lifted the canal some 40 ft above its natural water supply. Still, even with ten extra locks and a big, steam-operated pumping station, Jessop saved the canal company some £41,000.

Ray and his team spend the cold winter months maintaining Crofton's two Cornish beam engines, which regularly relieve British Waterways' electric pumps on summer weekends. The

older of the two machines was installed in 1812 and, says Ray with evident pride, 'it's the oldest working beam engine in the world. It's still in its original building; still doing its original job.'

Nearby Wilton Water was also built to service the canal's voracious appetite for water, but an easy stroll beside this charming reservoir reinforced my own craving for something rather more sustaining. The path led me to the tiny village of Wilton for a lunchtime rendezvous at The Swan. Over a plate of homemade duck sausages, I settled into conversation with John Talbot, an active member of the village windmill society.

Like Wilton Water, the windmill owes its existence to the canal, which re-routed the River Bedwyn and robbed the local water mills of their power supply. The mill, says John, is great fun – and the annual summer open day is a major event in the village calendar. 'All the children get involved, all the families. Everybody comes up to help… it's great!'

After lunch, we plodded steadily up the short hill for a closer look at the sturdy brick tower of the windmill that has dominated the local landscape since 1821. Flour was ground here for roughly a hundred years, John told me, after which the great sails hung motionless until Wiltshire County Council bought the mill and restored it to working order in the 1970s. Under the wide sky a hundred feet above the village, it's easy to catch his enthusiasm for this early example of renewable energy.

We said our goodbyes as the thin afternoon sunshine faded from the long misty ridges to the south. I set off past Hillbarn Farm up the forest road through Bedwyn Brail, a remnant of Le Broyle, one of the five bailiwicks of Savernake Forest. It was fast, easy walking; but, even so, the lights had come on in Brail Farm before I cleared the woods and dropped down to the canal at Great Bedwyn.

Back at the wharf, the morning's puddles were still frozen solid.

CAIRN ON SWIRL HOW, LAKE DISTRICT

WEST PENWITH, CORNWALL

SCILLONIAN ANCESTORS

Sam Llewellyn

I was born 30 miles west of Penzance, in the Isles of Scilly – one of the most beautiful landscapes in the world, never mind England. The islands are only rarely visible from the mainland. Until 170 years ago, they were indeed largely ignored, since they were useless for most mainland purposes, and the poverty of the inhabitants made them a less than pleasant topic of conversation, except for people engaged in periodic fundraising to relieve their suffering.

The islands lie at a crossroads in the sea. Ships homeward bound from the Atlantic paused there to pick up pilots for the Irish Sea, the Bristol Channel and the English Channel. If they were lucky. On a thick night, a mariner's first taste of Scilly was likely to be fog, strong breezes, a sudden steepening of an already enormous sea, a brutal crash of timber on granite, saltwater in the throat and oblivion. When day came, all that would remain were baulks of timber heaving in the Atlantic swell, and the long, narrow island gigs picking up wreckage.

The backdrop to these grim scenes was more like paradise than anything else to be found in England. The sand of Scilly is made of ground rock crystal, which gives it a curiously glittering whiteness, and paints the astonishingly clear water that overlies it with blues from palest turquoise to darkest indigo. The sea has carved the rocks into shapes splendid and grotesque. And it has warmed the islands to the point that they fall into a different climatic zone from the rest of the British Isles.

But in the early nineteenth century, nobody was looking at the view. The islands were out of sight and out of mind, devoted to smuggling, which in its danger and excitement occupied roughly the same place on Scilly as foxhunting on the mainland. The landlords, the Duchy of Cornwall, displayed an interest in the place directly proportional to the rent roll, which was negligible. The farms were poor and intricately subdivided, the islanders cut the scanty turf to burn in their fires, and in all the islands there was no tree higher than a gorse bush. In 50 years, most of the islands would be rocky deserts.

Then they attracted the attention of Augustus Smith, a rich young man who had fallen under the influence of the utilitarian moral philosopher Jeremy Bentham. Smith was looking for a place in which he could test his ideas. Scilly had no law, no money, no landlord to speak of and no opportunity to rise in the world. It was a blank slate on which Smith could write a prescription for the future. In 1834, he bought the lease and went to work.

To rationalise the farms, he evicted sub-tenants, who tended to be members of the tenants' families. He banned the burning of turf, arguing that if a farmer used his soil as fuel, there was little future for the farm. He introduced universal education 40 years before it became compulsory on the mainland – his version was not compulsory, but school attenders paid 1d per week and non-attenders paid 2d per week. The curriculum included mathematics, foreign languages and navigation. He made himself deeply unpopular, and was at one moment trussed in a sail and pegged out below the high-water mark to drown. Undeterred by this or anything else in the way of bad weather, insurrection, personal tragedy and expense, he built himself a mighty baronial house on Tresco, at the geographical centre of the archipelago. To this he invited large numbers of his friends for extended stays. If George III invented the urban seaside holiday at Weymouth and Brighton, there is a case for maintaining that Augustus Smith introduced the country-cottage version on Tresco.

But Smith did not enjoy living in a barren landscape. Scilly's winds make trees reluctant to grow. He rode the islands with a pocketful of gorse seed. Behind every young gorse bush he planted a tree. Behind the shelter belts thus formed he planted the Tresco Abbey Gardens, now one of the wonders of the world, 'Kew with the Lid Off'. His researches into ideal vegetation led to the adoption of pittosporum and escallonia as hedging plants, and the wind-hardy Monterey pine *Pinus radiata* as a shelter belt staple. In the newly-sheltered fields, a thriving cut-flower industry blossomed. Smith expended an enormous fortune on the islands and their people, and was rewarded in their transformation from a group of desert islands into something corresponding to most people's notion of the Garden of Eden.

Succeeding generations of Scillonians continued his work. But cut flowers are hard work in the face of government-subsidised Dutch greenhouses and flowers air-freighted from Kenya. A miraculous escape from the wreck of the deep-laden oil tanker *Torrey Canyon* pointed up Scilly's vulnerability to pollution

from the huge volumes of shipping that still ply this crossroads in the ocean. And the rape of the British seas by the French and Spanish fishing fleets has not helped Scilly's once-thriving inshore fishery. But all this has not marred Scilly. For a child, the islands were a paradise of clear water, bright sand, exotic birds and big fish, spiked with the dangers of deep sea, sudden weather and strong tides. Even now, each of the islands keeps its individual feeling. St Mary's, the biggest, the only one with cars on its roads, sometimes seems spiritually closer to the mainland than to the off-islands a mile or two across the sounds. Tresco is rather smart these days, with cottages for well-heeled holidaymakers, exquisite hotels and the legendary Abbey Garden. St Martins is quiet and funky and grows sweet-smelling flowers. St Agnes, westernmost of the inhabited islands, looks out at America through hedges of wave-battered rock spikes. And Bryher curls round the ghastly rocks of Hell Bay, much loved by holidaymaking poets. Actually, all Scilly's islands seem to have a talent for inspiring affection. If they had not attracted the affection of Augustus Smith, my ancestor, I would not have been born there.

RURAL RAILWAYS

The Right Reverend John Oliver

I t was love at first sight. I was 13 years old, and browsing in the library of the grammar school in Sussex when my attention was grabbed by a photograph on the front cover of a magazine – a photograph which, duly framed, still enjoys a place of honour in our retirement house, a permanent reminder of that conversion experience which was both instant and enduring.

The publication was *The Railway Magazine*, and the photograph was of the branch line train from Merstone, in the Isle of Wight, arriving at Ventnor West station, emerging from a jungle of lush summer foliage, on track where grass is growing vigorously between the rails. The locomotive is one of the beautiful little Terrier tank engines, built in the 1870s by William Stroudley for the London Brighton and South Coast Railway, which continued in active service with British Rail until the 1960s, and several of which survive in well cared-for preservation to this very day, well into the second century of their working lives. That picture cast a spell, and I remain a hopelessly addicted railway enthusiast, above all for the country branch line, served by elderly locomotives, equally venerable rolling stock, and patronised by only the occasional traveller.

Such branch lines no longer exist in real life, of course, although some of the 'Community Railways' which are enjoying something of a revival, manage to retain some characteristic branch line features. These lines are living proof of the continuing importance of the branch line railway in the twenty-first century. But this is an essentially nostalgic essay, and we can be thankful that on many of the preserved railways, such as the Bluebell and Severn Valley in particular, great efforts have been made to recreate the old authenticity: signalling, uniforms, platform furniture and so on, giving pleasure to people like me

who remember the branch line in its heyday with such affection, and also providing a form of living social history.

It may seem strange that I was not enthusiastic about trains from an earlier age – but I was a wartime child. The Battle of Britain was fought in the skies above Sussex where we lived, and the consuming passion of my early years was aviation. But I was lucky to be able to follow up my railway conversion by enjoying the railway scene where I lived. The famous photograph was of the Isle of Wight, and with severe petrol rationing in post-war years, long holiday journeys were impossible. Fortunately the Isle of Wight was within reach of Horsham, and it was only a year or two later that I spent a week with my long-suffering father and brother travelling on every one of the island lines (which then amounted to quite a system) with one of the Southern's famous holiday runabout tickets. The island trains, all steam hauled, immaculately clean and commendably punctual, offered a wonderful way of exploring the island, from Cowes to Freshwater, from Ryde to Bembridge and Ventnor, and there were splendid downland walks from many of the rural stations.

Perhaps this is part of the secret of the branch line's appeal. It threads through often beautiful countryside, opening up views at a gentle pace, inviting you to break your journey and wander off with a picnic on a summer day, rejoining a later train at a different station. Fifty years ago, the rural railway still played a very significant role in the local economy, conveying milk churns and farm produce, taking children to school, people to work and shoppers to market, as well as holidaymakers on leisurely journeys of exploration. There were charming branch lines from Horsham to Brighton and Guildford, meandering through the then empty landscapes of Sussex and even Surrey. A little further afield was the exquisite line from Pulborough through Petworth and Midhurst to Petersfield. There were quiet wayside halts, and also surprisingly grand station buildings, such as Christ's Hospital or Midhurst, eloquent testimony to the high hopes and ambitions of the railway builders – not often in practice fulfilled.

Rural railways fit surprisingly well into the landscape; because severe gradients must be avoided, they tend to follow the contours, and a line of track – even double track – takes up much less space than a modern road. Stand on Box Hill in Surrey, and notice how inconspicuous the railway is as it travels north towards Leatherhead and south towards Dorking, and then how harsh a scar is created by the A24. Or – even more dramatically – notice the contrast between the self-effacing nature of the railway through the Lune Gorge in the fringes of the Lake District compared with the monstrously ugly presence of the M6.

Over the years, I was able to explore by train almost every corner of England, and my railway enthusiasm undoubtedly added hugely to my understanding and enjoyment of history, geography and landscape. Railways provide a powerful sense of place, as the view from the carriage window changes from city centre to market town and to deep country.

The charm of railways is hard to analyse or explain. It partly depends on the quaint or archaic, but also on the fact that trains are both beautiful and functional, and railway architecture is often magnificent. There is a subtle relationship between order exemplified in timetables, track layouts and stock workings; and power. Even on branch lines, engines have to work hard against the gradient, and there is plenty of excitement in the insistent bark of the exhaust and the billowing smoke towering into the sky. When railways first appeared they were bitterly opposed by those who liked the landscape as it was. But now there will be many who are willing to echo John Betjeman's heartfelt words in his poem 'Dilton Marsh Halt':

> *And when all the horrible roads are finally done for,*
> *And there's no more petrol left in the world to burn,*
> *Here to the Halt from Salisbury and from Bristol,*
> *Steam trains will return.*

But meanwhile, as long as roads and cars are with us, what of the branch line in the twenty-first century? The story is not by any means one of continuous decline; since the savage cuts imposed by Doctor Beeching in the 1960s, surviving branch lines have in many cases prospered. The concept of the Community Railway was born on the Sheffield to Huddersfield branch line in 1993, and the idea grew rapidly. It involves the active and enthusiastic engagement of local people, working with professional railwaymen, to take forward local railways in both urban and rural areas in positive ways, by means of a cycle of modest improvements, operating the line in a simpler, more cost-effective way, introducing station adoption schemes, and driving up passenger numbers through local advertising and through arranging special events such as music trains and Santa Specials. One of the best things done by the Strategic Rail Authority in its brief and undistinguished existence was to recognise the potential of branch lines, and to appoint an 'Executive Director, Community Rail', with some funding and official support. Many lines, from the Heart of Wales to the Scottish Borders, from West Country to East Anglia and North Yorkshire, have seen their fortunes change for the better. The present tragedy, at the time of writing in spring 2006, is that the Department for Transport, under severe pressure from the Treasury, is threatening drastic new cuts to branch line services, undoing all that has been achieved in recent years.

MEADOWS, TRACKS AND BOUNDARIES

...it lies
Deep meadow'd happy, fair with orchard lawns
And bowery hollows...

Alfred Lord Tennyson, 'Morte D'Arthur'

MY SMALL CORNER
Robin Page

Cambridgeshire is not a beautiful county. It has suffered from excessive use of the plough and concrete mixer that some people call 'progress'. But tucked away, out of sight, is a field – an important field. It can be found at the end of a farm track and through a gate. It is a small field, barely three acres in size.

Along three sides are sprawling hedgerows, on the other is a lowland brook with old creaking willows and clumps of bramble. Once the brook was full of summer life and colour – yellow irises, marsh marigolds and flowering rush – and in winter, water would spill from its banks after every rain or thaw of snow. Then the dredgers came and lowered its bed; to the water engineers and cereal farmers it became a drain; it ceased to flood and the fields beyond its banks were ploughed, the hedges removed to grow wheat. A flood plain became a wheat field; meadows that once gave cowslips and birdsong were ploughed to create a grain mountain. But our small field remained. We kept the flowers and grasses, the sprawling hedges. We tried to restore the damaged brook with its plants of purple loosestrife and yellow water lily. Why did we do it? Because we wanted to do it – we felt it was our responsibility to do it.

It has not been a wasted effort for now, surrounded by prairies, beneath the flight paths of aircraft and within the roar of the restless M11 is an oasis – an oasis of beauty and sanity; a natural antidote to the madness going on around it. Three acres of birdsong and scent; colour, mood and calm in seasonal procession. With the spring comes the tumbling call of the willow warbler, falling and floating with the blossom petals of crab apple as bloom turns to pollinated fruit. A turtle dove

purrs by, its nest in an old thorn. Along the hedge unknown insects tell of another world before they are replaced by the more familiar butterfly wings of high summer – the gatekeeper, the speckled wood and the common blue. High in a willow, young hobbies peer over the edge of their nest as a fox in its fine summer coat hunts for voles. But the wings and paws that 'progress' drove away have come back through care, concern and action – white wings of the barn owl again drift over the meadow at dusk; otters glide easily through the water.

As late summer moves to autumn, the wild hedgerow harvest ripens – there are blackberries and sloes, hips and haws, crab apples and the scarlet berries of spindle. Large bats also appear on warm evenings – what they are and where they come from, I have no idea. It was a favourite field of Gordon Beningfield, the artist, and he would sit and sketch the hedgerow in full fruit. With falling leaves the naked berries turn the hedgerow red until the fieldfares and redwings arrive in hundreds to strip the branches bare.

Even when the cold winds of winter blow it is a warm field. The hedges give it shelter and a temperature several degrees warmer than its neighbours. It is like a walled garden – with the wall built from trees, branches and leaves – hawthorn, buckthorn, dogwood, ash, field maple, elder, small leaved lime and several more.

In the base of the hedge is a large flat stone – left when the ice retreated 10,000 years ago. It marks the spot where my old lurcher Bramble is buried and one day I will join him there.

But others have visited the field, too. On one occasion the Secretary of State, for agriculture, John Gummer, arrived,

wearing a suit and shiny shoes. 'What should I do?' I asked him. 'Over the hedge all the cereal farmers get subsidies for their prairie fields, but for this one we get nothing. We get nothing for producing birds, butterflies and flowers – is it inefficient? Should we pull up its hedges and plough its ancient grass? Should we be contributing to the European Grain Mountain?' 'No', he replied, 'it's a wonderful field – you must keep it as it is.'

Over the years, Britain has lost thousands of such fields – hundreds of thousands of such fields. When measured in acres, disappearing birdsong or butterfly wings, the total and the damage are enormous. But it is no longer an oasis. We have joined it with neighbouring fields that we have helped back to full life, where the plough and the combine harvester work together with nature, and skylarks sing over 400 acres, not just three. Amazingly, too, we now receive a subsidy for that little field, to help keep its wildlife, its character and its heart.

For me it is the most beautiful and important place in Britain.

COW PARSLEY, SUSSEX

One speaks of the moods of spring, but the days that are her true children have only one mood: they
are all full of the rising and dropping of winds, and the whistling of birds. New flowers may come out,
the green embroidery of the hedges increase, but the same heaven broods overhead, soft, thick and blue,
the same figures, seen and unseen, are wandering by coppice and meadow.

EM Forster, from *Howards End*

THE JOUSTING MEADOW

Jilly Cooper

Several times a week, I walk four dogs down the Toadsmoor Valley. In frenzied excitement, they charge down a tree tunnel out on to a grassy path. On the left is a field which has been turned into a sanctuary for rescued battery hens.

Chugging its way through marsh marigolds along the bottom of the hens' field is the Toadsmoor stream. On its banks tower balsam poplars which gently waft their sweet scent during the spring.

Following the stream through two gates and over a stile, we pass a lovely old mill before we reach the valley proper, a green ride which slopes steeply downwards for a quarter of a mile. Snorting joyfully, the old dogs break into a canter. The young dogs take off into the woods on either side. Undetectable against the fawns and umbers of winter undergrowth, the lurcher crackles maniacally through the pale ghosts of last year's hogweed, ragwort and nettle.

In spring, the ride, which has never been sprayed, is adrift with violets and primroses, whilst summer brings everything from scabious to spotted orchids growing thicker than buttercups.

In winter, the valley is lit by the sulphur blur of hazel catkins, and every 50 yards, like a street musician, a robin sings from the branches of a thorn tree. The grass is pockmarked by the hoofprints of a herd of Highland ponies. Rumbustious and inquisitive, they thunder down to frisk my pockets for carrots.

Having watched the Toadsmoor stream reduced to a trickle in the past, I can only rejoice at the recent downpours which have transformed it into a torrent, thundering louder than the ponies' hoofbeats. Crashing over logs and rocks, it vanishes every so often into caverns of bramble and wild rose.

At the bottom of the ride, the stream slows, choked by forget-me-nots, and the grass levels out into a sweep of flat land – a jousting meadow where perhaps medieval knights once battled for some beautiful lady. The surrounding woods are festooned with old man's beard, like some druids' amphitheatre. One can imagine the grey elders shuffling into their seats to gaze down on the knights tourneying below.

Leaving the jousting meadow and the stream to chatter down the valley, we fork to the right into a beautiful wood, where all around us logs and rocks are being re-upholstered in the acid green plush of spring moss.

We mount a path known as the nettle tunnel, because in summer it becomes too overgrown to walk through with bare legs; then up a field so steep it silences even the most relentless chatterbox. The climb is worth it, for turning at the top you can see the full glory of the Toadsmoor unrolling: khaki fields dotted with ash blond farms and crisscrossed by hedgerows. And on the great procession of bare trees that accompanies the stream down the valley can be detected the first garnet and amethyst glow of new buds as mist rises opal blue in a thousand smoke signals.

Completing the circle we plunge into the little wood which leads back to our house. Even on the very bleakest, greyest day, the path is lit by the beacons of little beeches still clinging to their red leaves. But already, bluebells, wild garlic, celandine and violets, sadly beloved of slugs, are thrusting their way through the sodden, russet leaf mould, and badgers are burrowing in the cocoa brown earth. Soon spring will join us on our walk.

ABOVE NASEBY, NORTHAMPTONSHIRE   **BELOW** SWALEDALE, YORKSHIRE DALES

RIGHT NEAR TOTNES, DEVON

FLOWERING GRASS

Peter Marren

I've always been a bit suspicious about the word green. When we say things like 'going green' or 'greening our lifestyle' it stands as a sort of code word for a healthy living and care for the environment. Yet there is nothing particularly healthy about an all-green landscape, a sea of plant chlorophyll. In Britain the nearest we have to an all-green scene is a field of rye grass, such as those which cover large parts of the Midlands, in which black and white cows stand out like billiard balls on a baize table. Here green is a negation of diversity. Green is about absence. It means no flowers, no seasonal colour, nothing but slick, sown grass living on chemical fertiliser. This is the green of dollar bills and old pound notes, and it has nothing to do with nature.

Living where I do in the upper Kennet valley, the view from my window embraces an expanse of grass that was the nearest the past could find to a field of rye grass. It is a water meadow. In the days before fertiliser came from the chemical works on Teesmouth, water meadows were perhaps the most genuinely green places in the whole countryside. They were, as far as possible, all grass. The meadows were irrigated by a series of drains which diverted river water onto the meadow, protecting the grass from frosts and feeding it with a sustainable dollop of silt every winter. Flowers were not encouraged. The system was too expensive to operate, needing the services of a skilled meadow manager called a 'drowner' who maintained the drains and sluices, and made the tricky decisions about when to pour the water on and when to take it off. In Thomas Hardy's day, the water meadows of Wessex were the equivalent of top-price, high-intensity arable land today. And they were run with no more sentimentality than a prairie farmer listening to the test score in his combine harvester.

But even so, as I look down on the meadow in the interminable late winter of 2006, it is not really green, or at least to call it green would be as absurdly reductionist as to say that a Rembrandt painting is brown. In fact a watercolourist would need the full range of his paintbox even in this eerily flowerless March. The corrugations formed by the parallel drains draw alternate bands of soft yellow-greens and browns. The afternoon light flickers on the straws of last year's grass which begin to glow as the sun sinks behind the wood. The blackish stems of rushes counterpoint the fawn tussocks of coarse grass with the sweet spring grass just starting to show between them. That at least is green, but it is not the bilious green of rye grass. It is more of a mellow April green, kissed with gold, a fresh, vibrant green to warm the heart after a long cold winter.

Once the spring is underway and the grass is growing up fast to form this year's hay crop, the meadow erupts into sharper colour. The yellow orbs of marsh marigold, which always seem to be at their brightest around May Day, dot the hollows and drains, while the later buttercups, cuckoo flowers and ragged robin add floating hazes of sunny yellow, lilac and pink (strange how a flower may be individually crimson but en masse become pink. Is it a trick of the eye?). Even the flowering grass is far from being simply green. The pollen-covered brushes of meadow foxtail fleck the grass stems with tawny brown, the aptly-named Yorkshire fog with greyish mist. Meanwhile, the almost permanent cool, westerly wind from the downs swirls the colour into motion in one of nature's psychedelic caprices.

Even the river has its painterly moment when it suddenly and most unexpectedly bursts into blossom. The upper Kennet is renowned for its unlikely rafts of white flowers born on deep-green wisps of spray. They belong to a plant that shelters the

young trout and oxygenates the water, and is as important to the river economy as the meadow grass is to the land. And yet it lacks an agreed name. River keepers call it *ranunculus*, which is latin for 'little frog', or just 'weed'. Flower lovers refer to it as 'crowfoot', while botanists, with a fine disregard of verbal economy, insist that it is the stream water-crowfoot, *Ranunculus penicillatus* subspecies *pseudofluitans*.

It needed the services of William Barnes, the dialect poet of Dorset (whose lines buzz like bees on a midzummer day) to bring to the river blossom a sense of what makes our hearts sing (or, as he would say, rather aptly, 'zing'). To him it was the 'small-feaced flow'r of sparklen zummer brooks... So fair upon the sky-blue stream/As whitest clouds, a hangen high/Avore the blueness of the sky.'

The sky reflected in the river by a flower: such are the quiet wonders of our understated wild flora. Compared with the pleasure we take in them, the literature of our wildflowers is fairly modest. The warnings of the conservation press, by contrast, are measureless and blaring. The zummer brooks sparkle less than they did, we are told, the water meadows are falling into decay and the brown trout have so much less *ranunculus* to cool their flanks.

It may be so. Perhaps we are all doomed, and the flowers along with us. But William Barnes, too, was living in a time of rapid agricultural change, though his instinct was to glance nostalgically back to past glories than to peer fearfully ahead into the unknown. Surely concern about conservation and the troubled climate need not withhold simple pleasure in the present. To enjoy wildflowers we need only to look at them, in their boundless colours, shapes and variety, and to let their sparkle sink into our old English bones.

And to stop supposing that nature is coloured green.

QUANTOCKS, SOMERSET

COMMON POPPY AND
OTHER WILD FLOWERS

...we slid through the glass and lay on our backs and just stared at the empty sky. There was nothing to do. Nothing moved or happened, nothing happened at all except summer. Small heated winds blew over our faces, dandelion seeds floated by, burnt sap and roast nettles tingled our nostrils together with the dull rust smell of dry ground. The grass was June high and had come up with a rush, a massed entanglement of species, crested with flowers and spears of wild wheat, and coiled with clambering vetches, the whole of it humming with blundering bees and flickering with scarlet butterflies. Chewing grass on our backs, the grass scaffolding the sky, the summer was all we heard; cuckoos crossed distances on chains of cries, flies buzzed and choked in the ears, and the saw-toothed chatter of mowing machines drifted on waves of air from the fields.

Laurie Lee, from *Cider with Rosie*

A PORTRAIT OF ENGLAND

QUIET LANES

Richard Mabey

The signs began to appear in the lanes around our house a few months back. They were slightly unearthly: a man, woman and child in silhouette, gazing up a winding track towards a single tree. They looked as if they were about to leave us for some far better place. Above them, written in elegant italic, were the words Quiet Lane. Nothing more. I wondered if, unwittingly, we'd been declared a Noise-Free Zone, or an Area of Special Consideration for Children, and a call to Norfolk County Council for an explanation led me to the Countryside Agency. They'd started the scheme back in 2000, as a measure to protect the character of some rural lanes, and to encourage equal status and consideration for all their users. The designation had legal standing, but no sanctions, and the signing was meant to be backed up my 'community consultation' and traffic redirection in the surrounding areas.

These bits of infrastructure seemed to have passed us by here, but I found I was beguiled by the signs. The domed heads of the family gave them a remote, Buddhist look, as if they had been parachuted in from Tibet, and each time I passed the silhouetted trio, frozen at the point of embarkation, I felt as if I ought to be taking off a hat, or my shoes, as if I were going through the gates of a shrine. Despite feeling we already have enough prescriptive paraphernalia in our country roads, I was being willingly ushered into quietude.

I rather enjoyed being encouraged to be self-conscious, to back off a little from the mayhem of first impressions, to taste quietness 'to', as much as quietness 'from'. Back in the 1970s, Kenneth Allsop wrote a piece in his mould-breaking country column in the *Daily Mail* about a walk amongst the west Dorset hills when 'absolutely nothing had happened'. Of course, just about everything possible had happened – in Allsop's head at least. Looking down from the great whalebone hulk of Eggardon, he sees, as if by time travel, the layers of the landscape unfurling, the puckered layers of chalk and sandstone, the Neolithic burial mounds, King John's hunting forest, the streams leading back to his own medieval mill-house.

Up in our Quiet Lanes today, it is not quite working like that. I'm on Norfolk's great arable plateau, and the wind, gusting in straight from the Urals, seems to be planing even the few tufts of vegetation flat. As a would-be quiet place, it is a sight too quiet. There is nothing for the wind to cleave to. Wood Lane and its wisps of hedge winds north-east. The Heywood is a smudgy settlement on the horizon. But not a hint of the vast hornbeam forest that grew here in medieval times remains. It is easier to imagine this empty desolation as the echo of some ancient marsh, though East Norfolk's Great Fen never spread to this altitude.

The stillness here doesn't resonate like Allsop's chalk bulwarks. It feels awkward, jagged, a hard geometry imposed on the land. Stepping back, it isn't human history that you feel rising out of the landscape, but rhythms of life that predate it, and still cut across it. In these few quiet weeks of stubble, streams of migrant birds move through this ephemeral oasis. There are larks, where there were none in spring. Black swarms of rooks gather in the dusks. High above, higher even than the lapwing flocks, the first golden plover are coming back to flock ranges probably established in the Stone Age.

The landscape is full of cryptic echoes. I walk up Algar Lane, past Nordle Corner – and there, squashed by the side of the road, is a tiny grass snake. The back of its neck is flashed with a brilliant lemon patch, a gratuitous tattoo. When I pick it up, the lovely dark suede of its body still twitches. It is only the second grass snake I have seen since I've been in Norfolk – about as many as the cars I've seen in this lane – and I wonder about the improbability of their paths crossing.

Quiet is about space as well as the absence of noise. The land is scribbled on by the movements and murmurings of countless beings. We need a quietness to hear them.

NORTH KENT DOWNS

A PORTRAIT OF ENGLAND

KENT

NEWS FROM SOMEWHERE

Roger Scruton

At a certain point in Stendhal's *Le Rouge et le Noir* the hero, Julien Sorel, makes a journey to England. He is appalled by the barbarous manners, lack of sophistication and the gross diet of the natives, and at the same time astonished by the one redeeming feature of their country, which is the indescribable sweetness of the landscape. And he seems to recognise what we all now know, that this sweetness is not the natural product of the soil, but the laborious and delicate by-product of centuries of peaceful settlement, in which fields and towns were hardly ever laid waste by warfare, in which independent farmers and settled landowners cared for their domains as trustees, and in which the rule of primogeniture ensured that farms, estates and villages passed on intact.

The most vivid symbol of this process is the hedgerow – which lays a living web of ownership across the land. In Slavonic languages a hedge is a *zhivy* plot – a 'living fence', though following communist collectivisation, few of them are left in the places where Slavonic languages are spoken. Not only are hedges alive, they also contain life – more life, perhaps, than the woods and converts that they join. They fill our crowded countryside with animals and birds, providing food, shelter and protection. Hedges are perhaps the most significant concession that man has made to other species, in his relentless search for territory. The hedge is also a symbol of community, a testimony to long-standing agreements over boundaries.

To be stockproof a hedge must be properly maintained. Where you see hedges that have grown straggly, with the trees wrestling upwards for the light, you know that the land is passing from the old grassland agriculture, in which sheep and cows were the main source of livelihood, to the new, in which horses, kept for the pleasure of urban refugees, have colonised the pasture. Horses are herd animals, but they do not move in a crush; each insists on its space, and defends it against encroachment. Hence horses can be confined to the flimsiest of wooden fences, while cows and sheep, which move in seething multitudes, will break down any barrier that is not able to withstand the combined weight of the herd. Where hedgerows are maintained, therefore, it is because of the business of meat and milk, which surrounds us here in the Wiltshire claylands. A properly matted hedge, armoured with thorns, and rooted over centuries, will withstand any number of panicking cows. Moreover, while a 'dead' fence is always getting weaker, a 'living' fence strengthens from year to year.

But when hedges have been allowed to riot upwards, they must be cut back and laid. Hedge-laying is a winter job, to be completed before the sap begins to rise. You need thorn-proof boots and trousers, a billhook for trimming, and a saw. You cut through the base of larger growths to within an inch of the bark, before pulling them down and binding them together, as near to the horizontal as you can. But you must know which to cut away entirely; which will be strong enough to form the central structure, which will encourage the hedge to grow inwards into its own mysterious darkness, instead of outwards to the light. Elms especially are a problem; do you bind them into the hedge, even if they are soon to die? Or is it true as some suggest, that Dutch elm disease strikes only when the tree has risen 20 ft above its roots, which it can never do when in a hedge? The old lore of hedge-laying – and there is plenty of it – is silent on this crucial point. But we have no choice; without the elms, our hedges would not exist, so we must lay them.

A rule of them, known after its inventor as Hooper's Rule, tells us that we should count one century for every species that a hedge contains (ignoring the brambles and climbers that come in from outside). Laying the hedge on Hanging Hill we have discovered black thorn, elm, ash, hawthorn, elder, crab apple hazel and privet. All our hedges deliver a similar count from which we assume that they we planted, not after the Enclosure Act, but it the early Middle Ages, when all this land belonged to Abbot of Malmesbury.

And this shows what boundaries have meant to the English. They are not there to assert absolute rights of ownership against the stranger, but to divide the land for husbandry. Impermeable to beasts, they are permeable to people, who enjoy footpaths and rights of way that link farm to farm across the hedgerows. The true rural boundary is not an absolute 'no' like the padlocked gate on the pony paddock; it is a qualified 'yes', the sign of a shared way of life and a common history.

HIGH PLACES

Return, musical, gay with blossom and fleetness,
Days when my sight shall be clear and my heart rejoice;
Come from the sea with breadth of approaching brightness,
When the blithe wind laughs on the hills with uplifted voice.

Siegfried Sassoon, 'To Victory'

High waving heather, 'neath stormy blasts bending,
Midnight and moonlight and bright shining stars;
Darkness and glory rejoicingly blending,
Earth rising to heaven and heaven descending,
Man's spirit away from its drear dongeon sending,
Bursting the fetters and breaking the bars.

All down the mountain sides, wild forest lending
One mighty voice to the life-giving wind;
Rivers their banks in the jubilee rending,
Fast through the valleys a reckless course wending,
Wider and deeper their waters extending,
Leaving a desolate desert behind.

Shining and lowering and swelling and dying,
Changing for ever from midnight to noon;
Roaring like thunder, like soft music sighing,
Shadows on shadows advancing and flying,
Lightning-bright flashes the deep gloom defying,
Coming as swiftly and fading as soon.

Emily Brontë, 'High Waving Heather,
'Neath Stormy Blasts Bending'

NORTH YORK MOORS NATIONAL PARK, YORKSHIRE

HIGH ON DARTMOOR
Wilfred Emmanuel-Jones

Like many people, in the 1950s my parents left the Caribbean to make their fortune in the Mother country. Because Jamaica was part of the then powerful British Commonwealth, many islanders wanted to come to England where they had heard that the streets were paved with gold, people lived in large houses and they had gas, electricity and water pumped straight to their house. No three-mile walk to fetch water before going to school. More importantly, there was work in abundance.

There was no milk and honey. For my parents it was only hard work, regret, a two-bed terrace – which had to house them, my eight brothers and sisters and I – and fond memories of their island home. But there was one place that encapsulated island life for my father. It was a paradise away from the concrete jungle that we lived in and it was a way of reconnecting with what he once was. His allotment was his pride and joy. When he was working on it, even if it was a cold midwinter day, as far as he was concerned he was back in Jamaica farming the land. This was when my father was at his happiest and as the eldest boy it was my responsibility to help look after this allotment. I too loved that place. I loved the sense of space, I loved the freedom, I loved being able to watch the vegetables grow. In the summer I would spend most of my time on the allotment. When I wasn't being disruptive at school this is where I would play truant.

So strong was the draw of this allotment and the open space it afforded that I had a strong sense that I had been there before. So much so that I made a promise to myself, at 12 years old, that one day I would own my part of the British countryside.

It took many years to keep the promise, but one fateful day on a trip to the West Country I took a wrong turn and ended up winding my way across Dartmoor. It was love at first sight and, eight years ago, it led me to buy a farm only a few miles away. I feel an affinity with the moor. There are no problems fitting in here, for everyone who visits is an outsider. I return to Dartmoor often – one particular walk, to Shavercombe Falls – keeps me coming back.

Man is afforded little compromise on Dartmoor. Here, nature has the upper hand, so it is no surprise to find man pitting himself against the challenges that Dartmoor sets. The Military, orienteers, school groups or just plucky individuals – all can be witnessed testing themselves here. If you can survive in this place, the feeling is that you'll be able to cope with anything.

I head for the River Plym following a track which eventually leads to what I can only guess is a condemned stone farmhouse – its boarded-up status gives a strong reminder that this place belongs to nature, not man.

Heading away from the farmhouse, Hen Tor proudly proclaims its right to be king of all it surveys. It looks as if it could have been put there by man, but its supremacy has been won by natural granite fighting endless battles against the elements.

Crossing Ditsworthy Weir sends a rush of blood to my head. You would think I was crossing the Niagara Falls; even a gentle flow of water concentrates the mind. There is less power flowing over this weir than I get from my bath tap, but because you can't turn it off, it automatically has my respect.

Walking along the river, its steady flow is mesmerising. Its understated persistence has had a massive effect on the landscape. As it finds its way, bending and twisting, its single objective is to get to journey's end – Plymouth. But I am heading towards its place of birth.

Looking towards the standing stones at Giant's Hill, long yellow grass fools the eye into thinking this is an expanse of desert being crossed by an army of oversized ants. It is only the bright pink shirts worn by a group of orienteers that allows the brain to compute that they are fellow human beings.

When I am forced a few yards away from the riverbank by boggy conditions, it is as if the river no longer exists. Hidden by tufts of springy grassland on either side, it fails to make its presence felt by either sight or sound.

The greatest motivation for moving away from the Plym is the pending change in scenery. Turning off to the right along Shavercombe Brook, the atmosphere is one of expectation as the banks rise higher and you are forced to pick your way along grassy and rocky ledges. Your senses signal that you are about to come across something memorable. Some 200 yards before you arrive, you are presented with a glorious scene, lifting the spirit.

Shavercombe Falls is tranquillity itself. Rock, vegetation and water live together in perfect harmony. It is an ideal spot to contemplate nature's wonders, to while away your worries, to recharge your spiritual energy – an altar at which man may find peace.

This heavenly place is difficult to leave, but leave one must, and for the rest of the route and then home I climb up high.

On a good day, I watch the sun and clouds playing peek-a-boo with each other, the shadows creating a spectacular display across the expanse of moor.

While the walk to the waterfall allows you to inspect the terrain up close, the return trip offers you the view of the gods. It is from here that you can see the river in all its glory making its imprint on the landscape.

It looks as if the River Plym is flowing uphill towards the sea. The landscape enjoys playing these tricks on the eye because you are in nature's playground and your rules don't apply.

As you're trying to work out whether the law of gravity is totally wrong, you are serenaded by a symphony of sound. It's important to be high up so you can hear this at its best. The wind is the first instrument you notice, then the distant waterfall reminding you of its pleasure recently given. Next, the crunching of dry grassland underfoot and, finally, sheep and their lambs introduce the vocals, intercepted by numerous birds rapping their own lyrics.

At journey's end, you find your senses more finely attuned than when you began the walk. The wonders and excitement of the trek widen your eyes and you have been blessed with most wonderful sounds, never heard in everyday city life.

The moors were even wilder than she had at first supposed. Like an immense desert they rolled form east to west, with tracks here and there across the surface and great hills breaking the skyline.

Where was their final boundary she could not tell, except that once, away to the westward, after climbing the highest tor behind Jamaica Inn, she caught the silver shimmer of the sea. It was a silent, desolate country though, vast and untouched by human hand; on the high tors the slabs of stone leant against one another in strange shapes and forms, massive sentinels who had stood there since the hand of God first fashioned them...

Strange winds blew from nowhere; they crept along the surface of the grass, and the grass shivered; they breathed upon the little pools of rain in the hollowed stones, and the pools rippled. Sometimes the wind shouted and cried, and the cry echoed in the crevices, and moaned, and was lost again. There was a silence on the tors that belonged to another age; an age that is past and vanished as though it had never been, an age when man did not exist, but pagan footsteps trod upon the hills. And there was a stillness in the air and a stranger, older peace, that was not the peace of God

Daphne du Maurier, from *Jamaica Inn*

BODMIN MOOR

A PORTRAIT OF ENGLAND

THE WITCH OF EXMOOR

Margaret Drabble

I have spent some of the happiest hours of my life walking on Exmoor. I first visited the West Country on a family holiday when I was a child, and I can still remember the intensity of my response to these new landscapes. I was brought up in Sheffield, and knew the Yorkshire moors and the Peak District from weekend outings, but there was something different about Exmoor that enthralled me. I love the steep combes, the astonishing sea views, the ancient woodland, the high open moorland. In 1989, we bought a house overlooking the Bristol Channel, and the Coast Path to Linton and Lynmouth goes just past our back gate. An evening walk up to Culbone church makes the best possible end to a day's work. I wrote my novel, *The Witch of Exmoor*, in part as a tribute to the scenes that had given me so much delight over the years. Scenes from Exmoor, North Somerset and North Devon tend to appear now in almost everything I write. They are part of my way of seeing.

The last stretch of coast road is of spectacular beauty. The sky above is still dazzling, but over the Bristol Channel below her, to her right, lies a fleece of white cloud, sucked up from the sun from who knows where, from the moorland, from the water. It rolls in innocent bundles, sparkling with light, and she flies above it, marvelling. To her left is the browned moorland, pricked yellow here and there with gorse, coloured a paler brown with the dried fawn cups and bells of heather, glowing the bronze of bracken: single thorn trees with a haze of red berries lean here and there from the prevailing wind. To her right is this sea above the sea, this strange and soft illusion. She knows that Wales lies out there across the channel, but although visibility seems infinite, she cannot see it. She feels has created the world afresh. No one has ever seen this world before.

The road unwinds before her and it glitters blue like water, blue like a thin high flowing river, as the tarmac reflects the sky. High carved copper hedges enclose her for a while and sheep gaze unmoved by the roadside. A cluster of ponies lift heads to watch her. Will she see deer on the hillside?

From *The Witch of Exmoor*

EXMOOR

HINDSCARTH AND SCOPE END, LAKE DISTRICT

BOWFELL FROM WRYNOSE PASS, CUMBRIA

OUR HUGE CHALK HILLS

David Dimbleby

I only know one small part of the South Downs which the Campaign to Protect Rural England (CPRE) has fought for so long to protect and preserve. I am lucky to live just below the north-facing slopes, a few miles west of Beachy Head, where the Downs finally slide into the English Channel. It is a steep 400-ft climb to the top, which protects it from crowds even on sunny summer days.

There are three ways up. To the east is the gentlest slope through rough meadow and past what look like terraces cut in the chalk, probably old chalk workings now covered with gorse and pitted with rabbit holes and badger setts. A scruffy walk this, which emerges on the side of the down and offers a tantalising glimpse of the sea. In the centre is the steepest climb, straight up to the top, often walking sideways using the sheep trails to keep a grip on the smooth turf. At the top of this walk, which I reach huffing and puffing, is what the map shows as a Neolithic burial mound and the sea, sometimes blue, but often a dramatic leaden grey streaked with silver where the sun finds a gap in the clouds.

Then there is the westerly route, passing woods which huddle at the foot of the Downs, eerie places where fallen trees have been bleached and eroded by sun and wind over so many years that they now look like the skeletons of giant fishes backbones, with a few spines protruding from them. From here it is another steep climb with pauses along the way to look across to Pevensey Bay where William landed, the marshes stretching across to Herstmonceux, the low Weald and the high ridge of Ashdown Forest behind. All three routes bring their own pleasure and sometimes I stand at the bottom while the dogs circle restlessly watching to see which way I will go, deciding which has the best light and which is protected from the wind.

There are deep purple violets half buried in the turf in spring, then thousand upon thousand of cowslips, and orchids sometimes out in the open, sometimes hidden in the woods. And always the skylarks, swooping up and hovering high above. Sometimes on a warm day I lie on my back screwing my eyes up against the sun searching for the source of the music, not satisfied until I see tiny brown wings beating manically.

The excitement of the Downs is that they are always changing. In their naked splendour they are susceptible to every nuance of light, different in every season and at every time of day. With a brilliant sun broken by cumulus racing across the sky they come alive, seeming to surge towards you as the light floods over them, Atlantic rollers climbing high above waiting to crash down and sweep you away. Gales from the south-west are so fierce you can barely climb the escarpment and if you are walking with a friend, buffeted and sometimes making no headway, you have to shout into their ear to be heard. And there are still days when drama gives way to quietness and the subtle shades of colour come into their own, every variety of grey and blue and green.

I can think of no better place to live, nor a luckier. In the crowded South East now steadily being eroded by housing and motorways and sodium lights, this small part of England is a reminder of what our countryside was like a hundred years ago. What matters now is not just to keep the South Downs free of development and as accessible as possible, but to devise new ways of using the land to protect it. Our huge chalk hills will never disappear, but the thin layer of soil that covers them is always at risk. Generations of farming has made them what they are. As the CPRE constantly reminds us, if the farming becomes unprofitable other ways of nurturing our landscape must be found – and nowhere more urgently than on these rolling hills which set us free.

THE LONG MAN OF
WILMINGTON, EAST SUSSEX

UPPER TEESDALE, COUNTY DURHAM

LANGDALE PIKE, LAKE DISTRICT

FOOD AND FARMING

The harvest moon has come,
Booming softly through heaven, like a bassoon.
And the earth replies all night, like a deep drum

Ted Hughes, 'The Harvest Moon'

THE SILENT VALLEY

WF Deedes

To me the future of rural England heavily depends on the outlook for farming; which is why I find the so-called new deal for farmers alarming. Broadly, they are to be paid not for the food they produce, but their stewardship of the land they possess. Do we grasp how fundamentally that alters their status and its implications for the countryside?

There are those, I know, who will take the opposite view, those who see farmers as enemies of rural England. Look at those ugly grain silos! Think of the hedgerows they have ripped out in the interests of intensive farming, to make way for their five-furrow ploughs and combine harvesters! Remember the chemicals they use to protect their wares and which threaten our health!

People who have recently moved to the country or have bought a second home there have a lot to say on those lines. OK, but I differ. It is farmers, warts and all, who have bequeathed us those rural skylines which we think of and treasure mainly when we are in distant lands.

Will they survive when farming ceases to be a productive industry? I doubt it. The woods, the fields, the silent valleys will not long survive the decline of farming. It's not dead yet, of course. A lot are going to soldier on for a while, for it's what they know best; but the tide is against them.

Man has always wanted cheap food. Supermarkets know that, and so do governments. So many farmers will come to realise that selling milk and meat at a loss is a mug's game; their main asset is the land they occupy. Some, I do not doubt, will use this asset intelligently, and at no loss to rural England. But others will go where the market directs, which is to provide homes and recreation for urban man. There is a big demand for those just now, and as the population of this island moves past the 60 million mark, it will grow.

When farmers had main responsibility for feeding the nation, they were influential people. They sat on county councils – and some still do. They had influence on the way we looked. No more. When the land ceases to be productive, to give us this day our daily bread, it becomes vulnerable. The Campaign to Protect Rural England (CPRE) has a fight on its hands.

MALVERN HILLS

STANDON, HERTFORDSHIRE

RURAL ROOTS

Jonathan Dimbleby

UNTIL THE END OF LAST YEAR (2005), MY HOME WAS A SMALL FARM THREE MILES OUTSIDE THE CITY OF BATH

Clinging to the edge of a steep valley at the southern tip of the Cotswold escarpment, the farmhouse lies just below the skyline and is sheltered from the prevailing westerlies by a stand of beech trees which runs along the ridge of the hillside. However, the land is 750 ft above sea level and – after we moved in – helpful locals told us that it was a 'two overcoats' sort of place, far colder than anywhere else around the valley. They were right, of course: when there is rain in Bath, we have sleet; when they have sleet, we have snow.

When a Low sweeps in from the west, we are frequently fogged in by cloud which clings to the homestead and depresses the spirits. Yet when there is a High, we sparkle under a clear sun from early in the morning and look down into a valley concealed by a blanket of white mist; we are above the clouds and the spirit soars. We listen intently to the weather forecast, not as the city-dweller for whom it is a form of entertaining self-flagellation, but more like seafarers for whom 'weather' really matters.

For those who delight in a rural landscape of hills and valleys, with ancient hedges that wind around small fields of gently differing tones of green – no violation in this valley by rapeseed yellow or linseed-oil blue – our outlook from north-west to south-east is quietly spectacular whatever the season: in spring, with the trees slowly coming into leaf, the sudden flowering of the hawthorn, the first cut of silage when the mower griddles new contours around the hillside and the smell of new grass wafts in the breeze; in high summer when the soil is cracked by the sun and the grass is parched, the combine throbs around the headlands devouring the first of the barley, the ash and the oak turn a darker shade of green, and calves and lambs, now strong enough to fend for themselves, still race to the maternal teat 'bunting' and sucking until the milk froths and foams from their lips; in autumn as the leaves start to whirlwind from the trees, when equinox gales drive the livestock to shelter behind wintering hedges, the plough turns the furrow and the hay meadows are rank with dying thistles; or in the damp chill of winter when the hillsides spurt water from hidden springs, the rooks huddle in the upper branches, and the wind sears through even the second overcoat. The cycle of life and death that is the essence of the natural world may be irredeemable and repetitive but, for me at least, it is a perpetual source of delight and wonder.

The price of a such a landscape is terrain that is unsuited to modern means of production. Our soil – grade 3 in the jargon – is too poor and the slopes too steep for large-scale arable cropping or milk production. Although four of our neighbours still contrive to maintain small dairy herds, most of the 11 farms in the valley are given over to beef production and all of them are run as small family businesses. Apart from the fact that our holding is run on organic principles, it is much like the rest except – a critical difference – that I do not depend on my farm for a livelihood. As a result, I am spared their perpetual anxiety.

For this reason, it would be fraudulent to regard myself as a genuine member of this embattled community. Although I farm seriously, it is my romance with the land which makes me do it and I know that I will not be ruined if I fail. Of course, I cling to the hope that, before it is too late, a wider public will come to cherish the concept of the small family farm and that no government will allow itself to preside over the strangulation of these dwindling communities. Yet, if there is no such awakening, I will be an observer of the process, not its victim.

SHEEP GRAZING

And that is what sets me apart from my neighbours, however sympathetic they know me to be about their predicament.

If my farm is an indulgence, I should explain, or rather explore, the character of this self-gratification. For a start, I like the company of animals, whether they are pets or farm animals bred and reared to produce milk or, in our case, to convert grass into meat. I enjoy watching our cows as they graze in the field, delighting in the slurp as a cow wraps her tongue around a tuft of grass and wrenches the green sward into her mouth. When the herd lies in a semicircle, a conclave of ruminants, collectively regurgitating the wet strands of nutrient from stomach to mouth and back to stomach again – chewing the cud – I allow myself the indulgence that they are 'contented' – and, as if by osmosis, I experience that emotion myself.

When a ewe strains in labour until the lamb's head finally appears, smeared in mucous and blood, and slithers suddenly onto the straw and the ewe rises at once to lick clean the nostrils and the mouth of her offspring, clearing away the detritus of her own afterbirth, nudging, nuzzling and nickering, until the frail, wet creature shudders into life – and though I have seen it again and again – I never lose the sense of wonder or that long moment of alarm until the lamb takes breath and struggles towards the mother's teat.

But our farm is not plagued by false sentiment. If it is fecund with new life, it also lives with death. If I rejoice when a lamb twitches its tail as it first suckles crucial colostrum from a fat teat, I have also delivered the rotting carcass of a dead lamb from the putrid womb of a dying ewe. If a newborn calf, half-buried in straw, steam rising from its flanks as its dam rasps at his head with her tongue, is a miraculous achievement, I do not forget that it is destined for the slaughterhouse, for that moment of final terror before it is hung, drawn and quartered for human consumption. When an elderly cow that likes to be stroked and has produced maybe 10 good calves in a life of perpetual nativity eventually proves barren, she is loaded into the cattle truck for despatch to the knacker's yard; there is no retirement, no rite of passage, no day of the dead. I may permit myself a lump in the throat or a tear in the eye, but I am constrained by the implacable truth that permeates my farm as any other: in the end agriculture is about life and death, beginnings and endings.

But if I resist false sentiment, I am not without romance. I am aware that this may seem absurd but, as I grapple to understand the emotions that a ripe cornfield or a herd of cows or a tractor on the skyline provoke in me, I can find no better – or more honest – term than 'love'. Of course, it is not that intensity of feeling which one human being may have for another in the first flush of passion or later when the fear of loss and the promise of grief overshadow every shared moment: you do not love a place on the map in the same way that you love a person – or rather, if you think you do, you are either deficient or deluded. But if you have ever caught your breath at the natural world, if you have ever ached to be by a favourite stream or meadow, if you have ever raged or grieved at the violation of a forest or copse to make way for an airport or housing estate or a bypass, if you heart soars when you see a hawk hovering or see a skylark on the wing, if the bark of a fox or scream of an owl stops you in your tracks, if you are mesmerised by a hoar frost or falling snow, if the moan of a high wind or the muttering from a thunder cloud fills you with awe, then you will understand that the term 'love' in relation to rural England is not as ludicrous as it might at first appear.

RETURN OF
THE PARTRIDGE

Peter Melchett

ORGANIC PIGS ROAM
FREELY AT PETER MELCHETT'S
COURTYARD FARM

On a wet September morning in 1935, seven people gathered at Courtyard Farm in North West Norfolk for a day's partridge shooting. Despite starting late, by lunch they had shot three pheasants, ten hares and a record 820 partridges. The day ended early, with the host saying 'This is too much like slaughter'. The head keeper, who wanted to carry on for the whole day, grumbled 'and we didn't get what we oughta'.

At that time, almost all the work on the farm was still done by people and horses. The Great Depression of the 1930s forced the Wharton family, who had farmed Courtyard Farm for three generations as tenants of the Hunstanton Estate, to sell up and leave. Raymond Wharton recorded every detail of the sale. He sold 27 horses, two foals, one mule, 13 cows, 641 sheep, 30 pigs and 159 chickens. The manure from all these animals provided the goodness needed to grow crops, and weeds and disease were controlled by the famous Norfolk four-course rotation, with different types of crops grown each year.

In 1935, when 820 partridges were shot, around 400 birds were present at the start of the spring breeding season. In the 1950s, when my father bought the farm, we still counted up to 400 English partridges each spring. By 1969, this had dropped to 50, and during the 1980s, the numbers went as low as 16 partridges. This extraordinary catastrophe for English partridges happened all over the country, and they became extinct in many areas. The number of most wild birds that depended on farmland for food and shelter also crashed. Animals that were common on Norfolk farms 50 years ago went into an astonishing decline, including hares, harvest mice, moles and butterflies. Wildflowers disappeared, too.

At first the gamekeepers, whose job it was to produce enough partridges for people to shoot, blamed the disaster on exceptional weather. I remember seeing dead partridge chicks on the farm as a boy in the 1960s and being told they had died of thirst. Wild animals have always had bad as well as good years, and it took until the 1980s for anyone in an official position to recognise that a disaster had taken place. This terrible loss happened because of a combination of changes of the last 50 years. After thousands of years of farming, only in the last 50 years have we used chemical sprays and artificial fertilisers. Mixed farms with animals and crops declined, factory farming and chemical use grew. Artificial fertilisers actually kill life in the soil. English partridge chicks need to eat insects in the first weeks of their life, and chemical sprays kill insects. So baby partridges, tree sparrows, corn buntings, yellow hammers and skylarks starve to death. Weed killers kill the native plants that hares and turtledoves depend on.

Fifty years ago, most crops were planted in the spring, and fields left over winter provided food for wildlife. Now most crops are planted in the autumn and the sprayed fields provide no food for wintering wildlife. So birds and other animals have declined because adults starve to death in winter, and their young starve to death in spring.

Many do not accept that modern farming has done all this damage, and have put the blame elsewhere. People walking in the countryside are accused of disturbing wildlife. More popular villains are magpies, crows and foxes. My experience at Courtyard shows that walkers, and predators such as magpies, are not to blame. Twenty years ago, we set up new public footpaths around the farm, and since then thousands of people have walked here every year. For the last 20 years, we haven't killed animals like stoats and weasels, foxes or jays, owls or magpies. If magpies or walkers were really responsible for the decline in wildlife, we wouldn't see many other birds on the farm.

In fact, over the last few years, we've seen wildlife return as we changed to organic farming. We have stopped using artificial fertilisers that kill life in the soil, and sprays that kill insects and weeds. Life has returned to the soil. Molehills back in our fields show that the worms that the moles eat are thriving again. The soil is providing insects for other wildlife to feed on, as well as goodness for the crops. We have four times the number of skylarks and three times the number of hares since we started to go organic. Autumn flocks of lapwing, golden plover and curlew are back, in greater numbers and staying longer than they have for 30 years. Green woodpeckers and barn owls breed on the farm for the first time in nearly 50 years. Migratory turtledoves are back on the north of the farm after an absence of 30 years.

In winter we now have fields of grass and clover, and fields sown with a winter covercrop. This holds the goodness for barley or wheat sown in the spring. All this means that we not only have more wildlife breeding on the farm in the spring and summer, but far more surviving the lean, cold days of winter.

During the last 50 years, much of the English countryside became a desert. Even at Courtyard Farm, where we planted new woods, put land aside for wildlife, restricted chemical spraying and kept beef cattle, the declines in wildlife continued. We have learnt this can be changed. Colour, movement and natural sounds can return to the Norfolk countryside with a new type of farming. This is not going backwards. Organic farming can produce as much or more than chemical farming, especially in developing countries. At Courtyard, we use the latest science. We have modern, safe and sophisticated machinery and, when we have to, modern medicines for our livestock (although the animals are so healthy that it's rarely necessary). Organic farming provides more jobs, far better welfare for farm animals, uses less energy and produces healthier, tastier food. What's more, it's food that local people seem keen to buy. We sell beef, pork and lamb through our village shop, to other village shops nearby, to the National Trust education centre on the coast, through two farm shops

and to our local primary school. Local sales benefit the environment and benefit the farm by giving us a diverse and reasonably secure income. A key to this is openness – anyone can walk round Courtyard Farm and see any of our animals any day of the year, and know that they will be killed and butchered within a few miles of the farm.

The English partridges at Courtyard Farm reached their low point of just 16 birds during the 1980s. We started to go organic in the 1990s and the number climbed to 40. In subsequent years numbers have gone as high as 90. We have a wonderful profusion of predators, foxes, stoats, weasels, crows, magpies and jays, all killed by gamekeepers years ago. This means we won't get back to the number of birds there were at the time of that record partridge shoot in 1935. But our experience shows you can have a modern, profitable farming system, producing healthy, good quality food, while bringing wildlife back to the British countryside.

NOT ON THE LABEL

Felicity Lawrence

In 1991, I came back to London after two years living in the Pakistani border town of Peshawar, working with refugees from Afghanistan's endless wars. My return to Western civilisation came via the supermarket, since in order to celebrate my homecoming, friends were preparing a special dinner. Shopping for it, as for most meals in industrialised countries these days, began and ended with a drive to the nearest big retailer.

I remember that shopping trip clearly because it was both exciting and, in some way I couldn't put my finger on at the time, vaguely troubling. I had been isolated from British culture for two years and I was experiencing the peculiar sense of dislocation that comes with seeing everything that was once so familiar as if for the first time. I was briefly glimpsing our food system from the outside.

Food from home is one of the things you most look forward to when you're abroad. I was almost drooling with anticipated pleasure as we drove past the boarded-up shops and cheap fast-food outlets in our high street. I had dreamed of sizzling bacon, soft smelly cheeses, fine wine and English chocolate. I chatted with my friend about the astonishing number of good foods you could find in supermarkets now, everything imaginable available in a one-stop motorised shop.

The damage to the landscape, the collapse of commodity prices, the exploitation of labour, the epidemics of disease and obesity, the concentrations of power we all worry about, are not the work of random or separate forces. The anxiety that has manifested itself in a succession of food scares is justified. I believe we are in the middle of one of the most significant revolutions since settled agriculture began 10,000 years ago. It is a revolution on a scale with the upheavals of our Industrial Revolution, both in its human and environmental impact. But this time it is global, not just national. It is a revolution whose social and ecological consequences we have so far failed to address.

AYLESBURY, BUCKINGHAMSHIRE

KENTMERE, LAKE DISTRICT

A FARMER'S LIFE FOR ME

Michael Morpurgo

There are three farms in Great Britain unlike any others, one in deepest North Devon, one on the Pembrokeshire coast in Wales, and one by the river Severn in Gloucestershire. On first sight they might look ordinary enough. Cows and goats are milked, sheep, pigs and calves are fed and watered, fields ploughed, corn drilled, apples picked, potatoes planted, hens and ducks and geese fed in the morning and shut up at night, barns are mucked out, hay made, cheese made, logs fetched in, potholes mended in the lane, straw harvested, sheep dogs whistled up. And on all these farms you'll see the farmer out working, on his tractor, walking his fields, busy about the farmyard. But he is not alone.

He has children with him, a dozen of them at least. They have come to help out on the farm. They come all around the year, a class at a time with their teachers, from cities and towns from all over Britain, children who have never seen the countryside close up before, who never felt it was theirs to go to, who have gone to the supermarket for their food and thought little about how it is produced. Now for a week of their school lives they are living the life of a farmer, working with him, doing everything they can to help run the farm, everything within the bounds of safety.

The work, as agricultural work is, is often hard, repetitive, dirty, uncomfortable – but they know it has to be done. It's what they've come for. The animals, the farm – they are the priority now. So it's up at 7am and out. It's a five-hour working day on the farm. They eat a lot, work a lot, play a lot, and they sleep a lot.

They go to bed tired. By the end of the week they'll know how milk is produced, what it takes to make a field of corn grow, why bees are necessary, why water is vital, why trees are life giving, where otters swim and badgers dig. They'll have watched buzzards soaring, larks rising, herons fishing, heard owls outside their bedroom windows, seen the black of night and the millions of stars up there. And they feel part of it all. They won't just be looking at it, they will be living it, doing the work, feeling the responsibility of it, and the pleasure and pain of it, witnessing new birth and death, cracking the ice on a puddle, feeling the wind on their faces, stomping through mud. How they love mud!

For these urban children this is a baptism of the countryside. Many leave thinking 'A farmer's life for me'. Many don't. But they all know now that this is their place, that they belong, that their work made a difference.

Farms for City Children, the charity that runs these three pioneer children's farms – real farms that have to earn their keep, not play farms, not tourist farms, but real working farms – is 30 years old this year. Begun by Clare Morpurgo and myself they are, we hope, the beginning of a longer story. For all children should have this experience in their lives, not just the 3,000 or so a year who benefit at present. The countryside of Britain can be a place for us all, our wildlife, our farmers and country people, for the recreation and education of us all, country people and city people alike. For children the countryside is simply the most wonderful resource, and woefully underused. Used wisely and sensitively, the impact of children on the countryside can be hugely beneficial, for employment for a start. But most importantly, children who have been to one of the farms and loved it, will realise just how precious the countryside is, how beautiful and useful it is, and how fragile it is, too, and that it is a work place and a play place. Long term surely this can only bring greater understanding between town and country, an understanding both badly need if the present divide between us is not to become an unbridgeable chasm. And that we simply cannot afford.

TRADITIONAL FARMYARD, GLAISDALE

Out of the wood of thoughts that grows by night

To be cut down by the sharp axe of light,–

Out of the night, two cocks together crow,

Cleaving the darkness with a silver blow:

And bright before my eyes twin trumpeters stand,

Heralds of splendour, one at either hand,

Each facing each as in a coat of arms:–

The milkers lace their boots up at the farms.

Edward Thomas, 'Cock-Crow'

RIVER ALN, ALNWICK

THE HUMAN CONNECTION

I was only going to say that heaven did not seem to be my home; and I broke my heart with weeping to come back to earth; and the angels were so angry that they flung me out, into the middle of the heath on the top of Wuthering Heights, where I woke sobbing for joy

Emily Brontë, *Wuthering Heights*

THE JEWEL GARDEN
Monty and Sarah Don

From the moment that we first visited the place in April 1988, I became consumed by the desire to transform the land around the house into a garden. I schemed, dreamed and planned constantly and, once we moved in, gave literally every spare moment to the project. I was 33 and in my prime. I felt fit and strong and had almost boundless energy. It was as though all the frustration of the London years was released onto this Herefordshire hillside.

I loved it there. From the first I knew I could happily spend the rest of my life there and, ideally, be buried on that hillside. This instant infatuation did not seem odd. I had had exactly the same sensation when I first met Sarah, despite her being married to someone else. I knew that she was the one. It took a little time and a divorce to sort things out, but I was right.

The place had little other than space to commend it. My response was entirely based on instinct. The garden had been used for many years to graze up to 30 horses at a time, effectively vandalising it. But it was indescribably beautiful, set on the steep hillside looking over the Frome Valley and across to the Black Mountains. A long drive flanked by a line of huge wellingtonias took you halfway up the hill to the house. Two thirds of our land was made up of fields too steep to cultivate. Orchids flowered at the top of the hill in June. Below the house it was wet and heavy with grass as lush as buttered asparagus.

When we arrived the docks were head high, brambles yards deep and elder sprouting everywhere. The first year I spent most of my time cutting things back. There was a five-acre mature orchard and next to that a two-acre wood where buzzards nested and foxes had an earth. We cleared much of the fallen timber and brambles and the following year thousands of primroses flowered under the trees. Along one edge of the wood was a ditch, which became a stream that ran into a clogged-up medieval fishpond. I unclogged it all and discovered a Victorian rockery. Now exposed, the mud started to sprout skunk cabbage, *gunnera*, *peltiphyllum*, rheum and irises.

I dug the old kitchen garden, adding the only good thing that in my book ever comes from horses – mountains of muck. We put up a greenhouse and some cold frames, and within a year were pretty much self-sufficient in vegetables. I made tree terraces where there had been a steep slope, moving hundreds of tonnes of rock and soil from one side of the house to the other. My favourite place to go if I needed to rest or hide was the orchard, where the owls also hid in the sprawling, unpruned apple trees during the day, their astonishing purple eyes watching from their branches. I would scramble up the steep bank with the dogs and sit under a tree, seeing everything in the valley and knowing that no one could see me. Then, when I was ready, I could go back down the hill to face the world again.

No-one else seems to have seen the sparkle on the brook, or heard the music at the hatch, or to have felt back through the centuries; and when I'm trying to describe these things to them they look at me with stolid incredulity. No-one seems to understand how I get food from the clouds, nor what there was in the night, nor why. It is not so good to look at it out of a window.

Richard Jefferies, from *My Old Village*

BAG ENDERBY, LINCOLNSHIRE

BROWNEY RIVER, DURHAM

THE DEMANDING LANDSCAPE

Bel Mooney

My life has come full circle now, and I am back in the town. First we moved from Clapham to a village near Bath to bring up the children, then to an organic farm to pursue some kind of dream – but now, 26 years on, I walk the city streets once more, and my old life (in every aspect) seems a long way away, even though the old farm is but a five-minute drive from my new townhouse. Yet the child who was brought up in a council house in Liverpool, who became the young woman who always crowed that she was 'a city person', has been permanently changed by the experience of living in the countryside. The limestone landscape I knew for a quarter century has shifted my perspective, so that I cannot but look beyond concrete and clay to another, more ancient and spiritual wholeness and the moral imperatives carried within every leaf. The nodding cowslips which so delighted me in our organic fields became indeed the keys to the kingdom. They opened the door to what we called 'nature study' in my Liverpool primary school, in an area where wildflowers did not exist.

The word 'nature' has many meanings, but central to them all is the idea that the 'natural' has its own life, unmodified by man. Nature untamed, nature red in tooth and claw, nature with its cycles of destruction and rebirth, nature in contrast to nurture, nature as evolution, nature as conscience, symbolised by the shot albatross... all these images flesh out the persona invoked by the demented King Lear, the 'great Goddess' of Nature he begs to hear his cause. Implacable, obeying her own laws, nature is. That blind, awe-inspiring power made primitive humans shiver, and inspired the Greeks and Romans to see gods in every tree, as well as in the fruitful fields and perilous oceans. It demanded terror and respect.

Two things stand in opposition to this vision of omnipotent nature: God and man. By God, I mean the giver of life the maker of heaven and Earth, for if life is 'given' how then can it evolve according to infinitesimal shifts of time? Bizarrely still discussed by American fundamental 'creationists' who deny Darwin, this was the question which shook the edifice of Victorian belief. If you see nature as the perfect manifestation of God's grace, made by the great designer, then for the believer it is an expression of divine will which must be subject to that will. As for man (and the masculine singular includes the feminine, since women are not guiltless; I deliberately employ the old-fashioned construction), his history is one of a continuous attempt to control nature, whether for convenience or survival. At its best this shows in the cultivation of garden, park and field, the domestication of animals and the development of medicine. At its worst, the assumption that man, centre of the universe, must bend it to his will, by (for example) the use of chemical pesticides and fertiliser, so that nature is perverted, its chains of dependence broken – with destructive consequences. This is the conviction that, created by God or not (and probably not), the natural world exists solely for the use of humankind, to be ruthlessly controlled.

If God and man, in their different ways, control Lear's rampant Goddess of storm and spirit, they command separate but equally powerful armies with which to subjugate her. One attacks through complacency, the other through commerce. Those who believe in a god-created world have always shown a tendency towards fatalism: war, famine, pestilence and flood may bring horror, but are, after all, a just punishment for man's sins, and so God's will be done. This is not so archaic as it sounds; back in the 1980s, it was fascinating to witness the attempts of some churchmen to justify the possession of nuclear

weapons, in spite of the wholesale destruction of man and nature they carry with them. It seemed they had no problem in accepting that God, who created the Earth, might allow man to destroy it. Similarly, those who place all their trust in man and his works are likely to put commercial interests before conservation – and thus we go on polluting the atmosphere, clearing forests, plundering the water courses, and so on, despite all the evidence which begs us to cease. The same people are also generally prepared to sanction the potential destruction of life to defend this or that political idea, or national borders – or any of the other human constructs which matter less than a single plankton matters in the mass of ocean life.

'L'homme propose, dieu dispose' will not do. We have no right to accept that some unseen will, or our intrinsic rapacity and ignorance prevent us from assuming responsibility for the future of the Earth. We have no choice but to accommodate

ourselves to the needs of the planet, for how can we expect it to accommodate itself to us, polluted, despoiled and threatened as it is? If we were to see ourselves as emancipated animals we could not conceive of allowing the environment which is our home to be destroyed by our own actions. We are a relatively small part of the natural world yet we are the part granted a moral sense; our duty is to use that sixth sense to listen to the silent messages in the very air that we breathe.

If this sounds both abstract and desperate, and many miles away from the countryside I love around Bath, I should say it is not. I had never thought about these things until I became, temporarily a country girl, and then – just by living, daydreaming whilst looking at the view, becoming heavily involved in a road protest and being exposed to the persuasive arguments of the organic movement – there was to be no going back. My starting point was always the particular history of my locality – a good springboard from which to leap into the larger world. History must needs foster humility, and the earnest wish to reconcile the needs of past, present and future. The past – whether represented by a patch of green belt or a crumbling church tower – requires our constant attention and respect, although many would deny that in the name of 'progress', the utilitarian needs of the now. So they still blast the natural world in the way Rachel Carson described in *Silent Spring* so many years ago: Monsanto still up to its tricks. And if a certain species become extinct, or a beach is polluted, or fish die through chemical waste... hush... protests are romantic or (worse) subversive.

The point about this gentle countryside is that it does not represent any escape from reality: the 'good life' dream of urbanites wishing to downsize and grow things. The countryside is under threat from the very people who romanticise it: they buy a cottage then demand street lighting so they can see where the monster 4x4 is going. No... my countryside forces you into a toughly realistic reappraisal of your own values. There is no escape: the sloping fields and munching sheep, even the recalcitrant nettles require you to think about your relationship with them. The quietness shouts at you to listen, and once you open your ears it will even whisper to you of the rainforests. Always the landscape imposes its identity on those who open up to it – as Wordsworth found when, as a boy, he tried to steal a rowing boat and imaged, in his guilty horror, that the mountain itself reared up to rebuke him. For the poet (and his contemporaries) nature was a moral force which served not just as a subject of aesthetic contemplation in itself, but was a teacher and a means to direct thought back to the still, sad music of humanity. The moral wellbeing of mankind and the spirit of the Earth were inextricably entwined.

This is because we cannot live without some contact with the natural world; it is essential to our spiritual wellbeing – or, more simply, to our happiness. That is why as many people still like to walk the Cotswold Way as to visit one of the horrible out-of-town 'designer outlets' and malls which have ruined both open spaces and town centres. When that is no longer the case... well... I hope I shall long have become a part of the shrinking countryside. If we are indifferent to the fate of a single hedgerow we have begun a process of spiritual withering, and at that stage there is no point in survival anyway. The joy that medieval people felt in the spring ('Sumer is icomen in...') at the end of the dark and bitter winter was surely no different in its essence from the sudden rush of pleasure city dwellers experience today at the sight of the first February daffodils in a municipal garden. Such sensations connect us through the centuries and transcend any technological fixes. They return us to dreams, visions, instincts, emotions and all the multifarious powers of the thirsty imagination. And all this implies no flight from logic or reason. On the contrary – it is an expression of the wisdom in the blood, instructing us in the most important lesson of all: humility.

I no longer own the cowslip meadows, but the hedgerows we planted will grow without us, and my awareness of the importance of plant life and hedges and ponds, of birds and insects and all the tiny systems of being, is a source of constant gratitude. The sheer glory of it all makes me understand what the poet Rumi meant: 'There are hundreds of ways to kneel and kiss the ground.'

TIN MINE, CORNWALL

VIRGINIA WATER, SURREY

TRANQUIL RESTORATION
Alain de Botton

Mand I left London by an afternoon train and travelled up the spine of England. The immediate motives for our journey were personal; but they could also have been said to belong to a broader historical movement dating back to the second half of the eighteenth century, in which city dwellers began for the first time to travel in great numbers through the countryside in an attempt to restore health to their bodies, and more importantly, harmony to their souls. We arrived at Oxenholme station, subtitled 'The Lake District', shortly before nine.

I had come in part because of a poet. William Wordsworth was born in 1770 in the small town of Cockermouth on the northern edge of the Lake District. He spent, in his words, 'half his boyhood in running wild among the Mountains', and, aside from interludes in London and Cambridge and travels around Europe, lived his whole life in the Lake District. Almost every day, he went on a long walk in the mountains or along the lakeshores.

It was during his cadeish walks that Wordsworth derived the inspiration for many of his poems, including 'To a butterfly', 'To the cuckoo', 'To a skylark', 'To the Daisy' and 'To the small Celandine' – poems about natural phenomena which poets had hitherto looked at casually or ritualistically, but which Wordsworth now declared to be the noblest subjects of his craft.

They were not haphazard articulations of pleasure. Behind them lay a well-developed philosophy of nature, which – infusing all of Wordsworth's work – made an original and, in the history of Western thought, hugely influential claim about our requirements for happiness and the origins of our unhappiness. The poet proposed that nature, which he took to comprise, among other elements, birds, streams, daffodils and sheep, was an indispensable corrective to the psychological damage inflicted by life in the city.

In the summer of 1798, Wordsworth and his sister went on a walking holiday along the Wye valley in Wales, where William had a moment of revelation about the power of nature, which was to resonate through his poetry for the rest of his life. It was his second visit to the valley; he had walked along it five years before and in the intervening period he had gone through a succession of unhappy experiences. He had spent time in London, a city he feared, he had altered his political views by reading Godwin, he had transformed his sense of a poet's mission through his friendship with Coleridge and he had travelled across a revolutionary France wrecked by Robespierre's Great Terror.

Back in Wye, Wordsworth found an elevated spot, sat under a sycamore tree, looked out across the valley and its river, cliffs, hedgerows and forests – and was inspired to write perhaps his greatest poem. At least, 'no poem of mine was composed under circumstances more pleasant for me to remember than this,' he later explained of 'Lines composed a few miles above Tintern Abbey', subtitled, 'On revisiting the banks of the Wye during a Tour. July 13, 1798', an ode to the restorative powers of nature.

> *These beauteous forms,*
> *Through a long absence, have not been to me,*
> *As is a landscape to a blind man's eye:*
> *But oft, in lonely rooms, and 'mid the din*

Of towns and cities, I have owed to them
In hours of weariness, sensations sweet...
With tranquil restoration

The dichotomy of town and country formed a backbone to the poem, the latter repeatedly invoked as a counter to the pernicious influence of the former.

　　　　　　　　　　　　　how oft,
In darkness, and amid the many shapes
Of joyless daylight; when the fretful stir
Unprofitable, and the fever of the world,
Have hung upon the beatings of my heart,
How oft, in spirit, have I turned to thee
O sylvan Wye! Thou wanderer through the woods,
How often has my spirit turned to thee!

An expression of gratitude that was to recur in *The Prelude*, where the poet once more acknowledged his debt to nature for allowing him to dwell in cities without succumbing to the base emotions he held they habitually fostered:

If, mingling with the world, I am content
With my own modest pleasures, and have lived
　　　　　　　　　...removed
From little enmities and low desires,
The gift is yours...
Ye winds and sounding cataracts! 'tis yours,
Ye mountains! thine, O Nature!

Why? Why would proximity to a cataract, a mountain or any other part of nature render one less likely to experience 'enmities and low desires' than proximity to crowded streets?

The Lake District offered suggestions.

In the Great Langdale valley, M and I were in deep countryside, where nature was more in evidence than humans. On either side of the path stood a number of oak trees. Each one grew far from the shadow of its neighbour, in fields so appetising to sheep that they had eaten them down to a perfect lawn. The oaks were of noble bearing, they did not trail their branches on the ground like willows, nor did their leaves have the dishevelled appearance of certain poplars who can look from close-up as though they have been awoken in the middle of the night without time to fix their hair. The oaks gathered their lower branches tightly under themselves while their upper branches grew in small orderly steps, producing a rich green foliage in an almost perfect circle – like an archetypal tree drawn by a child.

The rain, which continued to fall confidently despite the promises of the landlord, gave us a sense of the mass of the oaks. Standing under their damp canopy, rain could be heard falling on 40,000 leaves, creating a harmonious pitter-patter, varying in pitch according to whether water dripped onto a large or a small leaf, a high or a low one, one loaded with accumulated water or not. The trees were an image of ordered complexity: the roots patiently drew nutrients from the soil, the capillaries of their trunks sent water 25 metres upwards, each branch took enough, but not too much, for the needs of its own leaves, each leaf contributed to the maintenance of the whole. The trees were an image of patience, too, for they would sit out this rainy morning and the many that would follow it without complaint, adjusting themselves to the slow shift of the seasons – showing no ill-temper in a storm, no desire to wander from their spot for an impetuous journey across to another valley; content to keep their many slender fingers deep in the clammy soil, metres from their central stems and far from the tallest leaves which held the rainwater in their palms.

Wordsworth enjoyed sitting beneath oaks, listening to the rain or watching sunbeams fracture across their leaves. What he saw as the patience and dignity of the trees struck him as characteristic of nature's works, which were to be valued for holding up:

before the mind intoxicate
With present objects, and the busy dance
Of things that pass away, a temperate show
Of objects that endure

Nature would, he proposed, dispose us to seek out in life and in each other, 'Whate'er there is desirable and good.' She was an 'image of right reason' that would temper the crooked impulses of urban life.

To accept even in part Wordsworth's argument may require that we accept a prior principle: that our identities are to a greater or lesser extent malleable; that we change according to whom – and sometimes what – we are with. The company of certain people excites our generosity and sensitivity, of others, our competitiveness and envy. A's obsession with status and hierarchy may – almost imperceptibly – lead B to worry about his significance. A's jokes may quietly lend assistance to B's hitherto submerged sense of the ridiculous. But move B to another environment and his concerns will subtly shift in relation to a new interlocutor.

What may then be expected to occur to a person's identity in the company of a cataract or mountain, an oak tree or a celandine – objects which after all have no conscious concerns and so, it would seem, cannot either encourage nor censor behaviour? And yet an inanimate object may, to come to the lynchpin of Wordsworth's claim for the beneficial effects of nature, still work an influence on those around it. Natural scenes have the power to suggest certain values to us – oaks dignity, pines resolution, lakes calm – and in unobtrusive ways, may therefore act as inspirations to virtue.

EYAM, PEAK DISTRICT

A PORTRAIT OF ENGLAND

ENGINE HOUSE RUIN, WEST PENWITH, CORNWALL

ENCOUNTERS

Robert MacFarlane

Over the past three years, I have been travelling between the wilder landscapes of the British Isles. Wherever I have gone, I have found testimonies to the deep affection in which these landscapes are held. These testimonies have taken many forms. I have found poems tacked up on the walls of bothies. Benches set on lakesides or low hill passes, commemorating the favourite viewpoint of someone now dead. A graffito cut into an oak's bark decades previously, which had stretched and spread with the tree's growth, so that it looked like lettering on a balloon. Once, kneeling to drink from a pool near a waterfall in Cumbria, I found a brass plaque set discreetly beneath a rock: *In memory of George Walker/Who so loved this place.*

Such markers are the indicators of a process which is continuously at work in the British Isles: the drawing of happiness from landscapes. Happiness – and the repertoire of emotions which go by the collective noun of 'happiness': hope, joy, glee, wonder, surprise, calmness, and others. Every day, millions of everyday people find themselves deepened and dignified by their encounters with particular places.

Most of these places are not marked as special on any map. They become special by acquaintance. A bend in a river, the junction of four fields, a stretch of old hedgerow, or a fragment of woodland glimpsed from a road regularly commuted; these will do. So, too, will experiences: transitory, but still site-specific. A sparrowhawk sculling low through the sky. A cross-hatching of cirrostratus clouds. The fall of evening light on a boulder. A pigeon feather caught on a strand of spider-silk, twirling in midair like a magic trick. Daily, throughout the British Isles, people are brought to

sudden states of awe by encounters such as these: encounters whose power to move us is beyond expression, but also beyond denial.

Very little is said publicly about these encounters. This is partly because those who experience them feel no need to broadcast their feelings. A word is exchanged with a friend or partner; a photograph is kept; a note is made in a journal, a line is added to a letter. Many encounters do not even attain this degree of voice. They stay unarticulated, part of private thought. They return as memories: remembered while standing on a station platform packed tightly as a football crowd, or lying in bed unable to sleep, while the headlight beams of a passing car pan round the room.

The second reason why little is said about these encounters is that we find it hard, as a culture, to express this sense of what landscapes do to us. We have devised highly efficient metric systems for saying what they do for us: cost-benefit analyses of per-hectare yield, or tourist draw. But it is difficult to speak of their effects upon us without lapsing into the blithe or the mystical. And so, on the whole, we remain silent.

Yet, even as this great and legitimate process of consolation continues, so the landscapes capable of supplying it diminish. Over the last half-century, apocalypse has fallen upon the environment of the British Isles. The statistics of damage are familiar and often repeated, more as elegy now than as protest. In the last 50 years in England, fifty percent of hedgerow mileage has been grubbed up. Fifty percent of native woodland has been cleared, or replaced with conifer plantation. Ninety-seven percent of lowland grassland has been ploughed up, built over or tarmacked. Ninety

percent of heathland has been rendered into agri-prairie, or re-categorised as waste ground, and developed. One in five plant species is now classed as 'threatened'. Rare limestone pavements have been cracked up and sold as rockery stones, boglands have been gouged out and sold as back-garden peat. Rivers have become sumps for agri-chemicals. A tiny and dwindling proportion of mountain terrain is now more than five miles from a motorable road. Remoteness has been all but abolished. Wild land – in the radical etymological meaning of that word as 'self-willed land', land left entirely to its own devices – does not exist.

We live increasingly, as John Fowles wrote in 1970 , in the era of 'the plastic garden, the steel city, the chemical countryside'. We live in an era, too, when it has become in the interest of powerful commercial forces to erase the particularity of place, and to suppress the local distinctiveness of what landscape has survived modernity's onslaught. In an era in which the gap between knowledge and place yawns wider than ever before in the human history of this archipelago. In such an era, the vigilance and care of organisations such as the Campaign to Protect Rural England (CPRE), organisations which care for the land, and for its ability to console, restore and deepen, are of immense value.

DARTMOOR

AVEBURY

THE FUTURE

'*Oh, brave new World*'

William Shakespeare, *The Tempest*

UNPLANNED SPRAWL
Simon Jenkins

In the late 1990s, I travelled round England seeking its finest parish churches. I returned from each journey elated by the churches, but gloomy at the state of the landscape in which they stood. Each seemed besieged. The customary setting, of church, churchyard, cottages, high street and surrounding countryside was altering, not by the coherent accretion of planned settlement, but by the suburbanisation of modern estate housing. England, quite simply, was going the way of New Jersey or Connecticut.

When in the 1920s the writer, HV Morton, went 'in search of England', he did so on the assumption that England meant the countryside. He regarded rural as pure, goodly, timeless and English. Towns were dens of corruption and change. He wanted to see more townspeople journey to the country, to drink in its joys and absorb its value. His romanticism and fanatical conservatism seem quaint today. Yet they are privately adopted by millions of Britons seeking urban flight and hoping to colonise their chosen patch of rural Britain before the next wave of migrants follows.

Circumnavigate any large settlement in England and you will see a spreading stain of unco-ordinated, unplanned sprawl: round Ely and Peterborough, Nottingham and Derby, Cirencester and Cheltenham. The decline in the prospects of farming and the end of protection for 'prime agricultural land' leave everywhere outside a national park vulnerable to development. The newcomers demand changes to land uses, barns to warehouses, farms to estates, fields to caravans, garages and workshops to supermarkets. The community becomes a dormitory, in much of rural England a weekend dormitory.

This may be what people want personally. It is not what they want collectively. They want someone on their behalf collectively to control it. They want it planned so that what is recognisably rural is protected – 'listed' as we say of urban conservation – and new settlement corralled so that the boundary of town and country remains intact and people are encouraged to walk and meet in coherent communities, not drive and congest across a Milton Keynes grid of colonised landscape. This is common planning practice across Europe (no one is copying Milton Keynes).

I have absolutely no doubt that the present government is not of this mind. The free market ideas which have attached, rightly, to most areas of commerce have been extended into the one area where they can lead only to chaos, land-use planning. The Campaign to Protect Rural England (CPRE) claims that in the last two decades of the twentieth century, English rural land vanished under concrete at a faster rate than ever before. The loss of rural coastline – in Lincolnshire, Kent and Devon for instance – has been devastating. This has not gone to new towns located so as to preserve attractive coastline in between. Housing and caravans have simply been left to sprawl.

This has nothing whatsoever to do with the demand for housing. There is land aplenty, including derelict and old industrial sites, visible from any train journey or flight over England. There is absolutely no shortage of building land. There is a shortage only of the rural land which, by definition, housebuilders prefer and which, by definition, housebuilders render no longer rural. They and their market must be forced into planned settlements or England will simply become one extensive suburb.

There is no mystery and no doubt about where this is leading. It can be seen in the densely populated states of the American north-east. It can be seen in north Kent, in Essex, south Lancashire and in the uncontrolled development round Bristol. The future is before our eyes. I genuinely believe most Britons do not want it. But to stop it they will have to rise up and fight. The farming industry that once defended the countryside is being transformed by new forms of subsidy into new forms of activity. This is sustainable, but only if that activity is itself protected as essentially an activity of conservation. Rural England must do nothing short of redefine itself if it is to remain in anything like its existing form. I doubt if there has ever been a greater challenge to the geography of Britain.

NEW FOREST, HAMPSHIRE

HARTING DOWN, SOUTH DOWNS

THE WISEST USE OF LAND

Chris Baines

My lifelong love of nature has its roots in two contrasting landscapes. My parents were Sheffield ramblers so, long before I could walk, I was being carried shoulder-high across the Derbyshire Peaks. I have a particularly vivid childhood memory of being dragged through waist-high heather below Stanage Edge, with Dad insisting that we take no notice of the distant gamekeeper – so *mass-trespass* is in my genes. Passionate city dwellers played a vital role in creating national parks and other twentieth-century rural conservation landmarks.

The Peak District's heather moorland left me with a lasting love of wild and windswept open spaces. Nevertheless the urban landscapes very close to home have always been much more important to me on a daily basis. These are the landscapes that have really given me an intimate appreciation of the natural world. As a child I had no choice. Fishing for tadpoles, building dens and picking blackberries had to take place right on the doorstep. Even now, half a century later, it is still the downtown dawn chorus and the wilder side of town that offer me my daily dose of natural inspiration.

In my lifetime, the farming countryside has been abused on a heartbreaking scale, with habitat destroyed and once-familiar wildlife driven to the margins. By contrast, over that same period, England's urban areas have lost most of their polluting heavy industry and nature has re-established itself to a remarkable degree. Much of the so-called 'brownfield land' of post-industrial Britain now supports the bramble patches, shallow ponds and open, unsprayed grasslands that are so uncommon – and unwelcome – in our agricultural landscapes. No wonder farmland birds and butterflies that were a feature of the pre-war countryside are now much more familiar in the urban landscape.

I want the Campaign to Protect Rural England (CPRE) to keep campaigning for a green and pleasant countryside – but not at the expense of urban greenspace on the doorstep. Of all the people on Earth today, one in 100 live in the British Isles, and most live in cities, towns and suburbs. Research shows that close contact with wildlife and the changing seasons is the natural antidote to stressful modern life, which means protection of wild green places in our cities is all the more important. It would be a serious mistake to classify all England's unofficial urban open spaces as 'wasteland', 'derelict', or 'brownfields waiting for development'.

In such a crowded country there's a need to campaign for the wisest possible use of *all* the land. Of course when new homes must be built, it makes good sense to concentrate them in existing settlements, but only if we manage to retain their natural breathing places. Protecting rural England cannot mean the loss of parks and gardens, playing fields or naturally regenerated urban *wildspace*. It is these local landscapes that provide the daily opportunity to enjoy nature, play creatively or choose a car-free route to school or work. They constitute the functional green infrastructure that can filter air pollution, moderate storm water flooding and make urban living healthier.

In the long term, this unofficial countryside within the heart of towns is also vitally important for the wellbeing of rural England. Successful and sustained campaigning needs both popularity and passion. For me, and millions of others like me, that passion has its origins in nature on the doorstep. Lose that resource, and no campaign for rural England really stands a chance.

URBAN WILDLIFE HABITAT, RAINHAM MARSHES, EAST LONDON

A PORTRAIT OF ENGLAND

Encase your legs in nylons,
Bestride your house with pylons
    O age without a soul;
Away with gentle willows
And all the elmy billows
    That through your valleys roll.

Let's say goodbye to hedges
And roads with grassy edges
    And winding country lanes;
Let all things travel faster
Where motor car is master
    Till only Speed remains.

Destroy the ancient inn-signs
But strew the roads with tin signs
    'Keep Left', 'M4', 'Keep Out!'
Command, instruction, warning,
Repetitive adorning
    The rockeried roundabout;

For every raw obscenity
Must have its small 'amenity,'
    Its patch of shaven green,
And hoardings look a wonder
In banks of floribunda
    With floodlights in between.

Leave no old village standing
Which could provide a landing
    For aeroplanes to roar,
But spare such cheap defacements
As huts with shattered casements
    Unlived-in since the war.

Let no provincial High Street
Which might be your or my street
    Look as it used to do,
But let the chain stores place here
Their miles of blank glass facia
    And traffic thunder through.

And if there is some scenery,
Some unpretentious greenery,
    Surviving anywhere,
It does not need protecting
For soon we'll be erecting
    A Power Station there.

When all our roads are lighted
By concrete monsters sited
    Like gallows overhead,
Bathed in the yellow vomit
Each monster belches from it
    We'll know that we are dead.

John Betjeman,
'Inexpensive Progress'

SUSTAINABLE CITIES FOR A SUSTAINABLE COUNTRYSIDE

Richard Rogers

Cities are the framework of society, the generators of civic values and the cultural and economic command centres of our world. Twenty-first-century cities need to respond to our changing modern needs: they should be well-designed urban environments that encourage a broad mix of people living together with effective public services. And our needs extend beyond the metaphorical city walls, for ecologically, environmentally and socially sustainable cities can limit urban sprawl, and therefore help to prevent further erosion of our precious English countryside.

Three social changes are driving the need for urban renewal – the global information network with its effect on national barriers and the global market, the changing dynamics of family life with higher divorce rates, smaller families and increased life expectancy, and the twin demands of environmental responsibility and global sustainability. The only way, to my mind, we will reverse the drift of people from the city to the English countryside is by achieving urban regeneration through greater urban density and better design. We need a vibrant city of neighbourhoods, where people can live, work and play within walking distance. We must encourage new brownfield (not greenfield) developments, and the redevelopment of existing structures. We need clearly defined centres to limit out-of-town sprawl and expansion, integrated housing programmes and transport policies, and revitalised public spaces that create a strong sense of belonging and wellbeing, together with a balance of built form and nature. To create truly sustainable cities for now and for future generations, we also need fair distribution of justice, food, shelter, education, health, wealth and hope: and an economic framework that will generate and sustain employment.

Sustainable cities are compact, polycentric and ecologically aware, and achieving them should be our key aim. If we are successful, we can also hope to preserve and energise rural England.

URBAN SPRAWL, WEYMOUTH

DUNGENESS, KENT

CAMBOURNE, CAMBRIDGESHIRE

BRACED FOR CHANGE

Griff Rhys Jones

ifteen years ago, two books by great travel writers – Paul Theroux and Jonathan Raban – were published almost simultaneously. They both set out to circumnavigate Britain. One going by land, one drifting along by sea, they both went round in a state of woe, lamenting the picture windows and the ragged development and the insensitive roads littering the British littoral, and they both gave up on the far eastern shore. They got to Great Yarmouth and hurried back to London, leaving out the muddy mess of Essex and Suffolk altogether. They felt that there could be nothing of interest that close to London.

Interestingly, Raban repented. He wrote the foreword to his book in a cottage overlooking Rainham Marshes in a state of ecstatic conversion. He had discovered a secret. This area of creeks and waterways, flat islands and saltings, lifting fields and inaccessible peninsulas is a paradisiacal, conveniently forgotten hinterland. I don't want to write about it here. I don't want people to know that the banks of Essex estuaries can feel as remote as a Scottish loch. I don't want them to know that the valley of the Box is an unspoilt pastoral. I don't want them to know that, canoeing down the Stour, I have descended a magical river, scooping past trout, sliding over freshwater mussel shells glinting on the bottom, past garden-neat water lilies and bullrushes. Turning corners, pressing through woods, breasting hillocks, this landscape deftly reveals its surprises through lifted curtains. It doesn't blare it across an ice-age scoured mountainside. When I first came here, by boat with my father, we nosed up creeks feeling like Viking predators in a new country.

So why? How? Well, there was no coast road for Paul Theroux 20 years ago and there still isn't. Luckily there never can be. The coast is cut with marsh and inlet. The A12 has to run inland and the majority is too unadventurous to roam far from it. The banks of the estuaries are often privately owned. Walberswick, Aldeburgh and Southwold are popular now but were scorned in the past because they were dull. They are dull. The beaches are stony. There aren't many piers. The houses are undemonstrative. As a result they have become the most expensive in England.

We are urged to believe that our heritage will only be validated by tourism. Figures are produced that show that the rural environment or the restored country market town will pay for itself only if we encourage millions of visitors. But those who want to live by such figures will die by them. When the numbers don't add up, the grants can be withdrawn and anything can be justified. The only values that must be allowed to count are the values of evolved beauty and slow development. The countryside may be braced for change. It was ever thus. In the past, series of cataclysmic depressions have taken people off the land. Some will come back. There will be airports. There will be new buildings. There will be tourists. There will be stockbrokers living out here and there will be second homes. There will be businesses opening up and down country lanes. There will be converted barns. There will be new crops. They may be the end of hunting. There may be changes and amalgamations in agriculture. The urban people will come. The important thing is to look change in the eye and manage it well. We are not in a crisis. The rush to accommodate the lowest common denominator will kill what makes any of our countryside valuable. We need planned accommodation on the basis of difficult and diverse value, not fashionable ecological principles, not short-term economic panic, not desperate grasping at holistic, centralised solutions. Small is beautiful. Local is good. Individual imagination is paramount. Suffolk is slow. It has evolved that way, protected by its muddy creeks. Let it be so still.

BAMBURGH AT SUNRISE

MAKING OUR MARK

Dr Tristram Hunt

A HISTORIAN EXAMINES THE PAST, PRESENT AND FUTURE OF THE CAMPAIGN TO SAVE OUR COUNTRYSIDE

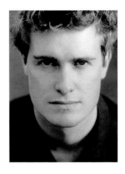

In 1933, Bradford-born author and broadcaster JB Priestley set out upon his *English Journey*. Leaving London along the Great Western Road, Priestley was transfixed by the never-ending sprawl of light industry, suburban housing, advertisement hoardings and traffic. Here was an England he had never experienced before. 'This is the England of arterial and bypass roads, of filling stations and factories that look like exhibition buildings, of giant cinemas and dance halls and cafés, bungalows with tiny garages, cocktail bars, Woolworths, motor-coaches… and everything given away for cigarette coupons.'

It was a determination to avoid this spectre which, 80 years ago, led a band of planning pioneers to establish the Council for the Preservation of Rural England. And by the time of Priestley's journey, CPRE had already started to demand development codes, National Parks, regulation of advertising and reforms to architectural design.

Since then, CPRE has transformed itself from an elite lobbying body into a popular pressure group with tens of thousands of supporters; it has moved from a close focus on design and aesthetics, to a broader concern with the social and economic levers driving rural change. It has also shifted from an amenity society to a more consciously environmental organisation. Yet, all the while, it has remained true to many of its founding ideals: a belief in the ecological and social importance of proper planning; an understanding of the vital inter-relationship between urban and rural; and a commitment to preserving the beauty, tranquillity and psychologically nourishing qualities of the English countryside for future generations.

CPRE was formed in 1926 in response to some of the greatest land use changes to the English countryside since the enclosures of the seventeenth century. The inter-war years witnessed a seismic cultural and political retreat from the dense urban ethos of the nineteenth century. Inspired by the Garden City and Suburb Movement, politicians and planners were unleashing the city onto the country.

The 1909 *Town Planning Act* signalled the shift from urban to suburban living. It was followed by an influential polemic from architect Raymond Unwin, *Nothing Gained by Overcrowding*, which passionately made the case for low-density, green-spaced garden suburbs. New homes for World War I heroes adhered to the suburban mould, and were then followed up by private developers who were exploiting strong housing demand on the back of historically low interest rates. The result was an avalanche of concrete. During the 1920s and 1930s, an average of 300,000 houses were built every year, with 1936 seeing a peak of 350,000. Overall, the inter-war years saw four million new houses go up, consuming 60,000 acres of rural land a year.

With them arrived modern car culture. Between 1924 and 1936, the price of the car fell by 50% and production increased by 500%. Previous geographical limitations on the growth of cities melted away as the car followed the tube, tram and train in prising open the suburbs of suburbia.

But at the same time as the urban tentacles were spreading, there arose a remarkable surge of interest in the English countryside and its meaning. This was the age of Edward Elgar and Ralph Vaughan Williams, of HV Morton and the search for England. Prime Minister Stanley Baldwin could

announce to universal acclamation that, 'To me, England is the country and the country is England.' Meanwhile, cycling, rambling, even folk culture enjoyed an unprecedented vogue among the broad middle class. By the mid-1930s, some 100,000 men and women were regularly hiking across the British landscape.

CPRE was a part of that naturalist turn, but at the same time managed to avoid its romanticist fringes. Very consciously, CPRE sought to differentiate itself from 'the sort of arid conservatism which tries to mummify the countryside'. By contrast, the Council's ambition was to ensure that through design, zoning and landscaping, progress did not irreversibly scar the English countryside. 'The development of this country is affected by all kinds of influences, arising from post-war conditions and new forms of transport,' remarked founding CPRE President Lord Crawford. 'We have got to have new roads and bridges, new suburbs, new villages, perhaps new towns. Our desire is that they shall be comely, and shall conform to modern requirements without injuring the ancient beauty of the land.' Modernist planner and CPRE guru Patrick Abercrombie asked, 'How much is it possible, owing to skilful planning... for the country to absorb without ceasing to be the country? How could it accept more buildings, new roads... and yet preserve its beauty?'

Yet if CPRE spurned a nostalgic revival of England, it was just as vehemently opposed to what Neville Chamberlain described as the 'spoiling of undefiled countryside by what is called the ribbon development'. This monstrous sprawl was the primary focus of the early CPRE, and its lobbying was rewarded in 1935 with the *Restriction of Ribbon Development Act*.

What this campaign against 'the dull uneventfulness' of suburbia opened CPRE up to is the long-running complaint that it was simply the working party of the landed wealthy. And there is little doubt that, during its first decade, the title-heavy CPRE was more concerned with preservation than public access. But to suggest natural heritage can only be appreciated by the leisured classes is to fall for one of the most reductive and philistine falsehoods.

Prior to World War II, the practical successes of CPRE were, in truth, quite limited. The combination of wartime patriotism and a cross-party belief in the virtue of planning changed all that.

During the conflict, CPRE was heavily involved in policy inquiries. This shifted the discourse about land management from a concentration on individual property rights to questions of collective heritage. At the same time, images of a pastoral England were central to propaganda on the Home Front. Added to this was the fact many Cabinet ministers had a background in the country pursuits culture of the 1930s. Labour Chancellor Hugh Dalton was nicknamed 'the Red Rambler' on account of his presidency of the Ramblers' Association.

The result was a welter of legislation dedicated to preserving the character of rural England, and preventing the planning mistakes of the inter-war years. The pinnacle was the 1947 *Town and Country Planning Act*, which remains an incredible legislative monument to the work of CPRE. A statutory obligation now existed for comprehensive development plans. Furthermore, the 1949 *National Parks and Access to the*

SALISBURY, WILTSHIRE

Countryside Act delivered CPRE's 20-year-long demand for protected National Parks along with Areas of Outstanding National Beauty.

But CPRE's work was by no means done. The governing ethos remained growth at any cost, as Government ministers combined with the free market to unpick planning restrictions. The Green Belt Circular of 1955 was a bright spot amid the Keynesian dash for motorways (such as the 1957 M1), industrial estates and out-of-town redevelopments. Moreover, a new threat had emerged within the countryside itself.

Much of the suburban growth of the inter-war years had been driven by collapsing agricultural prices and the abandonment of land due to international competition. During the post-war years, the situation reversed. British agriculture started to enjoy boom decades of subsidy and protection. A revolution in agricultural technology further spurred production and, before long, the mechanised, urban ethos was as much a product of the farm as the factory. Pesticides, tractors and guaranteed profits turned fields into prairies, and ensured the elimination of meadows, grasslands and hedgerows overnight. What dwindled rapidly alongside them were the farmland birds of England, as well as ancient agricultural signifiers of this island's history.

Better late than never, CPRE launched its Hedgerow Campaign in 1970, to chart their destruction and demand a system of preservation orders. In doing so, the Council (now renamed the Council for the Protection of Rural England) surfed the back of the environmental movement. While the original Council had boasted some of the leading botanists and naturalists of the day, design and aesthetics had often overridden environmental arguments. All that changed as CPRE fought the Manchester Water Order threatening the ecology of Ullswater and Windermere in the Lake District.

The environmental agenda only accelerated during the 1970s, as the Council helped defeat Southern Water Authority's highly damaging drainage scheme for Amberley Wild Brooks in West Sussex, as well as the attempt to convert Halvergate Marshes in the Norfolk Broads to arable production. In doing so, CPRE marked its transformation from an establishment-lobbying body to a more publicity-driven environmental pressure group. But while the public were listening, the politicians were not. The

1980s saw a shift back towards some of the worst laissez-faire planning policies of the 1930s. Green Belt rules were relaxed, out-of-town shopping centres encouraged, and so-called 'Roads to Prosperity' scythed through the Oxfordshire countryside and historic landscape of Twyford Down. Between 1980 and 2000, more open land vanished under development as a percentage of the whole than at any time in the twentieth century. The world of Priestley had returned, with a new generation of bypasses, and out-of-town mega-plexes. Valiantly, CPRE led a guerrilla campaign against deregulation ideologues and won notable victories on road routes, electricity and water privatisation, and the introduction of the long-fought-for Environmental Impact Assessments for major proposed developments.

Despite these sporadic successes, there were more powerful social and economic forces at work. The last third of the twentieth century saw the beginnings of the great counter-urbanisation of Britain. Hundreds of thousands fled Britain's cities as the end of industry and Empire gutted their commercial base. They fled to suburbia, exurbia and the edge cities, spilling into the countryside, suitably distant from the deserted inner cities. The Handsworth and Toxteth riots of the mid-1980s were only the most visible responses to an urban culture in crisis.

To its credit, CPRE had, by the early 1990s, positioned itself at the forefront of these urban debates. Declining, sprawling cities, with no sense of civic pride or municipal cohesion, were an enemy of the countryside. The Council's pamphlet on *Urban Footprints* made the ecological case for sensitive civic regeneration. Its support for New Urbanist thinking and assault upon the car culture helped provide the political context for the Government's 1995 retreat on out-of-town shopping centres, as well as more recent guidance on higher density design for new housing and the landmark Planning Policy Guidance: *Housing* (PPG3) promoting brownfield, mixed-use development.

But just as the depredations of laissez-faire planning seemed to be coming under control, CPRE (since 2003, a Campaign rather than Council) found itself battling the old enemy of unsustainable statist planning. Current schemes for a massive expansion of airports and housebuilding, particularly in the South East of England, have rightly been questioned by CPRE. The 2004 Barker Report, commissioned by the Treasury, demanded a 'step change' in housebuilding, with the rate of

land release for new homes predicated upon the local level of house prices. By contrast, CPRE stressed the need for affordable homes for local people and the necessity of developers providing proper community services rather than dumbed-down market houses in commuter-belt sprawl. At the close of 2005, the Government declared it wanted housebuilding rates in England to rise to 200,000 new homes a year – a level last sustained about 25 years ago – but at least it rejected the Barker mechanism of linking local land release to house prices.

As well as questioning the arithmetic of Barker's analysis, CPRE also opposed it because of the cumulative consequences of rampant housebuilding on the rural environment. As such, this reflected a shift towards campaigning over more intangible, 'quality of life' issues. The effects of noise, visual clutter and, above all, light pollution were progressively destroying the beauty, tranquillity and diversity of rural

England. A rash of road signage, the hum of bypasses and motorways, and the blinding of the night sky by careless, often needless outdoor lighting were undermining the distinctive qualities of country life. CPRE further developed this approach by working with the National Trust to stress the importance of power of place within local communities: the need to preserve those signifiers of land, history and culture within the urban and rural environment which help people to understand their heritage and identity in an ever-more transient and clone town Britain.

Extending that sense of distinctiveness to economic activity in rural areas remained an equal priority. Throughout the 1980s and 1990s, CPRE kept up the pressure on reform of the Common Agricultural Policy (CAP) in order to build in biodiversity and sustainable farming into its subsidy structure. Today, the future of farming goes right to the heart of debates about the countryside. The CAP Single Farm Payments system and Environmental Stewardship scheme has finally recognised the ecological case for countryside management. But more fundamental issues about the viability of UK farming within a global trade system, and the significance of food production relative to the leisure and landscape values of the countryside, require deeper analysis. In an era of climate change, big questions will need to be asked about the importance of long-term, national food security – and what that implies for farmland. Thus far, CPRE has rightly stressed the importance of niche agriculture production – regional, value-added, environmentally sensitive – but whether or not that constitutes a credible future for the sector as a whole remains uncertain.

This discussion points to more fundamental questions for today's CPRE. In a modern, multi-cultural, multi-ethnic Britain, it is no longer instinctively the case that the country is England and England is the country. People's identities are more diffuse, layered and often trans-global. Reaching out to a predominantly urban generation, is a difficult challenge when it comes to nurturing a constituency for conservation. At the same time, England's rolling countryside and market towns offer ever more attractive destinations for a wealthy middle class let down by urban schools and seduced by the pastiche of rural life on offer in Sunday newspaper supplements and *Escape to the Country*-style TV shows. All this racks up rural house prices, puts pressure on greenfields and leads to new socio-economic stresses within the countryside.

As such, CPRE faces new strategic challenges. It needs to confidently champion its rural base, but for influence's sake cannot afford to be regarded by Government Ministers as the cultural kin of the Countryside Alliance. With an area the size of Southampton disappearing under concrete each and every year, CPRE should be proud on occasion to be counted as a NIMBY (Not In My Back Yard). But it would be betraying its founding mission and making a strategic blunder by being labelled a BANANA (Build Absolutely Nothing ANywhere At all).

However, these are relatively minor positioning issues in contrast to the great opportunities which CPRE faces. After decades of dissimulation and dithering, planners and politicians are at last waking up to the significance of climate change. Housebuilding, roadbuilding, sprawl and airports are great drivers of increasing 'greenhouse gas' emissions which are causing global warming. The message which CPRE has been honing since the days of Abercrombie and Chamberlain is now more important than ever. Sustainable development, a co-ordinated strategy designed to limit the impact of the urban footprint, must be the basis for future planning policy.

More fundamentally, CPRE has the chance to channel the growing public appetite for history and heritage into its campaign to promote and protect rural England. The collapse of so many traditional social identifiers in modern Britain – class, religion, cohesive labour markets – has led to ever greater numbers bereft of a sense of belonging in time and place. Increasingly, people have turned to genealogical and local historical research to fill that void. Coupled with this is a growing popular interest in design, locality and the quality of place. But one of the most compelling elements of our heritage is the countryside: its landscapes, landmarks, artefacts, wildlife and wilderness, which all connect to deeper rhythms within our history.

It was the idea of natural and human heritage combined, which first inspired the founders of CPRE some 80 years ago.

Today, that modern connection to a past constitutes a decisive calling card for CPRE. As the assault on the English countryside continues – with urban sprawl replacing ribbon development; advertising hoardings showing up alongside motorways; Green Belt land under threat; and an inter-war-style avalanche of housebuilding looming – the mission and mandate of those pioneering, progressive preservationists remains more compelling than ever.

DR TRISTRAM HUNT is a lecturer in history at Queen Mary, University of London. Previously, he was an associate fellow at the Centre for History and Economics, King's College, Cambridge. His academic expertise is in nineteenth- and twentieth-century British cultural and urban history. He is the author of the critically acclaimed *Building Jerusalem: The Rise and Fall of the Victorian City* (Weidenfeld & Nicolson). A regular broadcaster and journalist, he recently authored a Channel 4 programme on Victorian civic pride and writes columns for *The Guardian* and *The Observer*. Tristram Hunt is a Fellow of the Royal Historical Society and a trustee of the Heritage Lottery Fund.

SUPPORT OUR CAMPAIGN

Shaun Spiers, Chief Executive, CPRE

SINCE 1926, THE CAMPAIGN TO PROTECT RURAL ENGLAND HAS FOUGHT TO PROTECT THE BEAUTY, LIFE AND UNIQUENESS OF OUR COUNTRYSIDE. WE LED THE CAMPAIGNS TO CREATE NATIONAL PARKS, AREAS OF OUTSTANDING NATURAL BEAUTY, GREEN BELTS AND THE TOWN AND COUNTRY PLANNING SYSTEM

CPRE is a registered charity with over 60,000 members and supporters across the country. We work as a network with over 200 district groups, a branch in every county, a group in every region and a National Office in London. Over 2,000 parish councils and 800 amenity societies also belong to CPRE, making us a powerful combination of effective local action and strong national campaigning.

Since our formation, CPRE has campaigned for a beautiful, tranquil and diverse countryside that everyone can value and enjoy; a working countryside that contributes to national wellbeing by enriching our quality of life, as well as providing us with crucial natural resources, including food. The countryside, including its villages and towns, is ever changing, but we strive to ensure that change and development respect the character of England's natural and built landscapes, enhancing the environment for the enjoyment and benefit of all.

Our work, as a national organisation, is to highlight threats to the countryside and promote realistic, constructive solutions, using in-depth research, lively campaigning, reasoned argument and lobbying. After 80 years on the job, have we succeeded? Is the glass half full or half empty?

Considering England's high population density and the huge growth in population and prosperity since 1926, one might conclude that we have been very successful. Despite being one of the most built-up countries in Europe, England still has huge tracts of diverse, very beautiful countryside which remains at the heart of our national identity. Many millions of people from the UK and overseas treasure our rural landscapes.

But even though CPRE's campaigning has slowed the rate at which countryside is being lost to sprawl, some 20 square miles of fields and woods disappear under paving and buildings each passing year. The countryside is under threat from housing developments; from new transport infrastructure, especially roads and airports; from noise, air and light pollution. Farming is under pressure to become ever more intensive and productive in order to meet globalised competition, yet we expect farmers to carry on serving as the leading custodians of the countryside. And climate change is coming; its first effects are already with us.

Looking back over the past 80 years, we find plenty to celebrate. But we continue to face enormous challenges from powerful organisations and interests which give rural landscapes no priority against profits and competitiveness and consumerism. We have a tough fight on our hands to ensure that England has a real countryside left eight decades from now. Please take a moment to consider giving us some support.

Campaign to Protect
Rural England

CAN YOU HELP US?

BY SUPPORTING CPRE, YOU
CONTRIBUTE TO THE CONTINUED
EXISTENCE OF A BEAUTIFUL, TRANQUIL
AND DIVERSE COUNTRYSIDE FOR
EVERYONE TO ENJOY. YOU CAN HELP BY:

- making a donation, or regular donations

- becoming a member of CPRE – and getting
  involved as much or as little as you want.
  Members receive our attractive thrice-yearly
  magazine *Countryside Voice* with news and
  features by leading writers about the modern
  countryside and CPRE's campaigning. Members
  can also obtain discounted entry to over 200
  houses and gardens across England

- becoming a volunteer with your local CPRE
  branch, many of which organise events as well
  as campaigning at the local level. We provide
  our volunteers with help and information

- leaving us a legacy

Find out more about how you can help by looking
at our website, **www.cpre.org.uk** and the *support
us* section **www.cpre.org.uk/support-us/index.htm**.
Or you can email us at
supporterservices@cpre.org.uk. Alternatively,
telephone our Supporter Services Team at
020 7981 2800 or write to Supporter Services,
CPRE, 128 Southwark Street, London SE1 0SW.

CONTRIBUTORS

CHRIS BAINES is one of the UK's leading environmentalists. He is an award-winning writer and broadcaster and he earns his living as an independent adviser to industry and to central and local government. He is a trustee of the Waterways Trust, a national vice president of The Wildlife Trusts and of the Countryside Management Association, president of the Thames Estuary Partnership, the Essex Wildlife Trust and the Urban Wildlife Network, and a recipient of the RSPB annual medal for services to conservation.

JILLY COOPER is a journalist, writer and media superstar. She is also the author of many number one bestselling novels, including *Riders, Rivals, Polo* and *Pandora*. Her latest novel, *Wicked!* is a tale of two schools. Jilly lives in Gloucestershire with her husband Leo and five cats. She was appointed OBE in the 2004 Queen's Birthday Honours list for her contribution to literature. She is a passionate lover of the countryside.

ALAIN DE BOTTON was born in Zurich, Switzerland in 1969. He published his first book at the age of 23. *Essays in Love* was a novel, but he has since moved into a genre of novelistic non-fiction. His books include *The Art of Travel, How Proust can change your Life* and *The Architecture of Happiness*.

WF DEEDES, Journalist since 1931

DAVID DIMBLEBY has been a broadcaster mainly with the BBC since the early 1960s. He is at present chairman of BBC's *Question Time*. Prior to that he presented *Panorama* for a number of years and has anchored every General Election since 1979. He has also made a number of documentary films: *The history of the Afrikaner: The White Tribe of Africa; An Ocean Apart* about Anglo-American relations; and films on India and the history of Rhodesia/Zimbabwe. In October 2004, he started work on *A Picture of Britain*, a six-part series for BBC 1, in conjunction with an exhibition at Tate Britain. The book *A Picture of Britain* derived from the series became an instant bestseller.

JONATHAN DIMBLEBY is a writer, broadcaster and film-maker. He presented ITV's flagship weekly political programme, *Jonathan Dimbleby*, and has presented *Any Questions?* and *Any Answers?* for BBC Radio 4 since 1987. He is vice-president of the CPRE and president of Voluntary Service Overseas; Bath Festivals Trust; Soil Association and Royal Society for the Protection of Birds. Jonathan is also trustee of the Richard Dimbleby Cancer Fund, Dimbleby Cancer Care and the Susan Chilcott Scholarship.

MONTY DON has presented gardening and travel programmes for 15 years and now presents BBC2's gardening programme, *Gardener's World*. He is a prolific journalist and has been *The Observer*'s gardening editor for the past ten years. He has written many books, including the prize-winning *Sensuous Garden* and the *Complete Gardener*. SARAH DON has studied architecture and design and has written many cookery columns. She and Monty have gardened, lived and worked together for 25 years and have collaborated on numerous projects, including the highly acclaimed book and Channel 4 series, *Fork to Fork*.

MARGARET DRABBLE was born in Sheffield in 1939 and educated at a Quaker school and at Newnham College, Cambridge, where she studied English literature. After a brief career as an actress with the Royal Shakespeare Company she became a full-time writer, and has published 16 novels. Her work has been translated into many languages. She edited the *Oxford Companion to English Literature* and her latest novel is *The Sea Lady*, set largely on the north-east coast. She lives in London and west Somerset.

WILFRED EMMANUEL-JONES is a farmer and businessman who sells high-quality meat from the West Country as the Black Farmer, a brand name invented by his farming neighbours. He also runs the Black Farmer Rural Scholarship Scheme, which enables young people from inner cities to experience countryside living and livelihoods.

RALPH FIENNES was born in 1962 in Suffolk, the first of six children. His father, Mark Fiennes, was a photographer and his mother was the novelist, painter and travel writer, Jini Fiennes. His film credits include *The Constant Gardener, Schindler's List, The English Patient, Quiz Show* and *Spider*.

SIR RANULPH FIENNES is an explorer who has been at the forefront of many exploratory expeditions since 1969, when he led the British Expedition on the White Nile, and has since led 22 major expeditions to remote parts of the world. He is also the author of 16 books, including *The Feather Men, Beyond the Limits* and his latest, *Captain Scott*. Sir Ranulph has, through his expeditions, raised large amounts of money for charities and was awarded the OBE in 1993 for 'human endeavour and charitable services'.

DAVID FOSTER is a freelance writer and photographer. He has written travel and general features for *The Daily Telegraph, The Times, The Independent* and *The Daily Express*, as well as contributing to numerous magazines and the regional press. He is also the author of several books, including *50 Walks in Surrey* (AA) and the Jarrold Short walks guide to the Isle of Wight.

ROY HATTERSLEY is a politician-turned-writer and broadcaster. He has been Granada Television's 'What the Papers Say' columnist of the year and in 2003 was elected a Fellow of the Royal Society of Literature.

SIMON JENKINS is a journalist and author. He writes a column for *The Guardian* and for *The Sunday Times*, as well as broadcasting for the BBC. Previously he wrote columns for *The Times* and the London *Evening Standard*, both of which newspapers he edited. He was deputy chairman of English Heritage and a Millennium Commissioner. He was Journalist of the Year in 1988 and Columnist of the Year in 1993. His books include works on London architecture, the press and politics and, more recently, *England's Thousand Best Churches* and *Thousand Best Houses*.

GRIFF RHYS JONES presents *Restoration* on BBC2. He is a comedian, writer and broadcaster, and was best known for *Not the Nine O'Clock News* and *Alas Smith and Jones* on BBC1.

FELICITY LAWRENCE is *The Guardian*'s consumer affairs correspondent and author of the bestselling exposé of the food industry *Not on the Label*. She spent two years working with refuges on the Afghan/Pakistan border in the early 1990s, following a stint as editor of *The Sunday Telegraph*'s colour supplement.

PENELOPE LIVELY spent her childhood in Egypt, but much of her adolescence in west Somerset – her memoir, *A House Unlocked*, was prompted by her grandmother's home there. She is a novelist and short story writer; her novel, *Moon Tiger*, won the Booker Prize in 1987.

SAM LLEWELLYN is a CPRE member. He was born in the Isles of Scilly and has spent large portions of his life on the sea. He has written dozens of novels for adults and children, and his journalism appears in *The Times*, *The Telegraph* and yachting magazines. He has recently written *Emperor Smith: The Man Who Built Scilly*, a biography of Augustus Smith.

RICHARD MABEY's latest book, *Nature Cure*, was shortlisted for the Whitbread Prize. He lives in Norfolk and is vice-president of the Open Spaces Society.

ROBERT MACFARLANE's first book, *Mountains of the Mind* (2003), about landscape and the imagination, won the Guardian First Book Award and the Somerset Maugham Award. He is presently writing a book about wildness and the British Isles. He is a Fellow of Emmanuel College, Cambridge, and writes regularly on literature and the environment for *The Guardian* and *The Sunday Times*.

PETER MARREN is the author of 16 books of natural history and related subjects, including *Britain's Rare Flowers* and *The New Naturalists*. He contributes to *The Daily Telegraph* and *The Independent*, and regularly to *British Wildlife*, *BBC Wildlife* and *Plantlife*. He previously worked for the Nature Conservancy Council as its inhouse 'author-editor'. He lives in the Kennet valley overlooking a water meadow.

JONATHAN MEADES is the author of three works of fiction, the most recent of which is *The Fowler Family Business*. He has written and performed in many television films on predominantly architectural matters such as Stalin's buildings, the utopian avoidance of right angles, Victorian architecture's debt to laudanum and tertiary syphilis and the lure of vertigo.

PETER MELCHETT is policy director of the Soil Association, the UK organic food and farming organisation. He runs an 890-acre organic farm in Norfolk, with pigs, beef cattle, sheep and arable crops. He is a member of the BBC's Rural Affairs Committee and the government's Organic Action Plan Group, and was a member of the Department of Education's School Lunches Review Panel.

GEORGE MONBIOT is the author of the bestselling books *The Age of Consent: a manifesto for a new world order* and *Captive State: the corporate takeover of Britain*; as well as the investigative travel books *Poisoned Arrows*, *Amazon Watershed* and *No Man's Land*. He writes a weekly column for *The Guardian*.

BEL MOONEY is a novelist, children's author, journalist and broadcaster. With around 30 books to her credit she is currently working on a new children's book, and developing broadcasting ideas, as well as writing a weekly column in *The Times*. She lives in Bath.

MICHAEL MORPURGO was the Children's Laureate from 2003-2005. He has published over one hundred books which have won prizes and been translated all over the world. With his wife Clare, he founded the charity Farms for City Children in 1976. So far over 60,000 city children have spent a week of their school lives down on the farm.

DR RICHARD MUIR is the author of around 50 books, mostly on countryside history/archaeology and he has written many articles about landscape history. He is an Honorary Research Fellow in geography and environment of Aberdeen University and an Honorary Life Member of the Yorkshire Dales Society.

ADAM NICOLSON is the author of many books on history, travel and the environment. He is the winner of the Somerset Maugham Award and the British Topography Prize and lives on a farm in Sussex.

THE RIGHT REVEREND JOHN OLIVER was the 103rd Bishop of Hereford from 1990-2003. He held three major rural conferences in Hereford, which led to the publication of a report entitled *Farming and the Catering Trade – linking producers to consumers*, which set out the valuable part which the church could play in rural affairs. He retired in 2003, to Powys in Wales, where he became assistant Bishop in the Diocese of Swansea and Brecon, and also Chairman of the West Midlands Rural Stress Support Network, Chaplain of the Royal Agricultural Benevolent Institution, and a non-executive director of the Rural Regeneration Unit.

ROBIN PAGE is a farmer, writer and conservationist. He lives on the Cambridgeshire farm where he was born and intends to stay there. He is founder and Chairman of the Countryside Restoration Trust, a charity

promoting wildlife-friendly farming on its own network of farms. He is addicted to village cricket and has travelled widely, particularly in Africa.

LIBBY PURVES is a writer and broadcaster who has presented *Midweek* on Radio 4 since 1984 and formerly presented the *Today* programme. She is a main columnist on *The Times* and in 1999 was named the Granada 'What the Papers Say' Columnist of the Year, and awarded an OBE for services to journalism.

RICHARD ROGERS is one of the foremost living architects, recipient of the RIBA Gold Medal in 1985, the 1999 Thomas Jefferson Memorial Foundation Medal and the 2000 Praemium Imperiale Prize for Architecture. He was awarded the Légion d'Honneur in 1986, knighted in 1991 and made a life peer in 1996. In 1995, he was the first architect ever invited to give the BBC Reith Lectures and in 1998 was appointed by the deputy prime minister to chair the UK government's Urban Task Force. He is chief adviser to the Mayor of London on architecture and urbanism and also serves as adviser to the Mayor of Barcelona's Urban Strategies Council. He best known for such pioneering buildings as the Centre Pompidou, Lloyd's of London and the Millennium Dome.

ROGER SCRUTON is a philosopher and writer. Formerly professor of aesthetics at Birkbeck College, London and visiting professor at Boston College, USA. He now lives as a freelance writer in Wiltshire. He has published *The West and the Rest*, *News from Somewhere*, *Gentle Regrets* and *A Political Philosophy with Continuum*.

TIM SMIT is chief executive and co-founder of the Eden Project in Cornwall. He is also a trustee, patron and board member of a number of statutory and voluntary bodies both locally and nationally. Tim is the author of books about both the Lost Gardens of Heligan and Eden, and has contributed to publications on a wide variety of subjects.

ALAN TITCHMARSH is a gardener, an author and a broadcaster. He has just completed his sixth novel, and is working on the second volume of his memoirs, having written nearly 40 gardening books. He is about to start filming a new BBC natural history series, which will take him all over the British Isles, yet he confesses he is never happier than working in his garden.

ACKNOWLEDGEMENTS

Extract from *The Jewel Garden* by Monty and Sarah Don reproduced by permission of Hodder and Stoughton Limited

Extract from *Jamaica Inn* by Daphne du Maurier reproduced by permission of Curtis Brown Limited

The Way Through the Woods by Rudyard Kipling reproduced by permission of Louise Lamont at AP Watt

Extract from *Cider with Rosie* by Laurie Lee reproduced by permission of The Estate of Laurie Lee and Penguin Books

Extracts from *Not on the Label* by Felicity Lawrence reproduced by permission of Penguin Books and Felicity Lawrence

'How the harmless wanderer in the woods became a mortal enemy' by George Monbiot reproduced by permission of Syndication at *The Guardian*

Extract from 'Dart' by Alice Oswald reproduced by permission of Peters, Fraser and Dunlop Limited

'Winter Seascape' and 'Inexpensive Progress' by John Betjeman reproduced by permission of Candida Lycett Green

PICTURE CREDITS

We'd like to thank all of the photographers and photographic agencies who have generously supported CPRE and the publication of *A Portrait of England* by donating pictures for use in the book.

4	CPRE/Derry Robinson	74	CPRE/Derry Robinson	120	Roderick Field
10	CPRE/Derry Robinson	75	CPRE/Derry Brabbs	121	CPRE/Julian Anderson
11	CPRE/Derry Robinson	76	Bob Langrish	125	CPRE/Martin Trelawney
12	Jonathan Buckley	77	CPRE/Derry Brabbs	122	CPRE/Derry Robinson
13	CPRE/Derry Robinson	78	Top: Michael Westmoreland	123	CPRE/Derry Brabbs
14	CPRE/Derry Robinson		Bottom: www.britainonview	126-127	Lee Frost
15	CPRE/Derry Robinson	79	CPRE/Derry Robinson	128	Ross Hoddinott/naturepl.com
17	CPRE/Derry Brabbs	81	NTPL/Andrew Butler	129	www.britainonview.com
19	CPRE/Derry Brabbs	82	CPRE/Derry Brabbs	130	Nicola Browne
20-21	CPRE/Derry Robinson	83	Chris Gomersal/naturepl.com	131	Darren Core/Alamy
23	CPRE/Derry Brabbs	84	Lizzie Orcutt	132	Britainonview/Martin Brent
24-25	CPRE/Derry Robinson	85	CPRE/Derry Brabbs	133	CPRE/Derry Robinson
27	Richard Coomber/Natural Visions	86	© MPL Communications Ltd 1987. Photographer Linda McCartney	134	Robin Allison Smith
29	CPRE/Derry Robinson			135	CPRE/Clive Arrowsmith
31	Steve Atkins /Alamy			137	CPRE/Derry Robinson
33	CPRE/Derry Brabbs	87	© MPL Communications Ltd 1985. Photographer Linda McCartney	138	CPRE/Derry Brabbs
36-37	NTPL/Paul Wakefield			139	Graeme Harris
38	CPRE/Derry Brabbs			140	Charlotte de Botton
39	CPRE/Derry Brabbs	89	Howard Rice	141	Heather Angel/Natural Visions
41	CPRE/Derry Robinson	90	Derry Brabbs	143	Heather Angel/Natural Visions
43	CPRE/Derry Robinson	91	www.britainonview.com	144	CPRE/Derry Robinson
45	NTPL/Derek Croucher	93	CPRE/Derry Brabbs	145	Bob Croxford
46-47	Lee Frost	95	CPRE/Denis Waugh	148	James Osmond
48-49	CPRE/Denis Waugh	97	Ross Hoddinott/naturepl.com	149	James Osmond
50	Charlie Waite	99	CPRE/Derry Brabbs	150	CPRE/Derry Brabbs
51	CPRE/Derry Brabbs	102	Francesco Guidicini/Rex Features	151	CPRE/David Rose
53	CPRE/David Rose	103	Britainonview/Martin Brent	152	Dan Chung/*The Guardian*
54-55	Lee Frost	104	CPRE/Derry Brabbs	153	James Osmond
57	Image © Nick Meers	105	CPRE/Derry Brabbs	154-155	CPRE
58	CPRE/Derry Brabbs	106	CPRE/David Rose	157	David Levenson (rspb-images.com)
61	NTPL/David Levenson	107	CPRE/Julian Anderson		
63	Stephen Davis/Alamy	109	CPRE/Derry Brabbs	161	Skyscan.co.uk/© John Farmar
64	Derry Brabbs	110-111	Britainonview/Rod Edwards	162	CPRE/Derry Robinson
65	Bob Croxford	112	R A Smith	163	CPRE/David Rose
67	Alex Ramsay	113	© MPL Communications Ltd 1987. Photographer Linda McCartney	164	Stuart Clarke/Rex Features
69	Railphotolibrary.com			166-167	Lee Frost
70	CPRE/Derry Robinson			174	CPRE/Derry Brabbs
73	CPRE/Derry Brabbs	118-119	Michael Westmoreland	177	Graeme Harris

CALOR IN YOUR LOCAL COMMUNITY

CALOR HAS BEEN PART OF THE RURAL LANDSCAPE FOR OVER 70 YEARS. THE COMPANY WAS ESTABLISHED IN 1935 BY A GROUP OF FARMERS TO MEET THE ENERGY NEEDS OF CUSTOMERS IN RURAL AREAS – AND THIS FOCUS HAS REMAINED CENTRAL TO THE BUSINESS EVER SINCE.

Calor continues to use its presence in, and understanding of, rural communities, not only to identify and develop an ever increasing range of applications for liquefied petroleum gas (LPG), but also to help rural communities to remain healthy, vibrant and sustainable.

This commitment to sustainability is central to Calor's culture and the company is proud of its track record of engagement with customers, employees and the wider public through long-standing relationships with organisations such as CPRE and Business in the Community (BITC). Communities and local businesses have also benefited from its strong links with other groups including ACRE and Forum for the Future, alongside work with charities such as the Fairyland Trust, Gardens for Schools, Childline and the Plunkett Foundation's Rural Revival Campaign.

CALOR VILLAGE OF THE YEAR®

Calor has supported rural activities in England, Scotland and Wales for 20 years through its Rural Sponsorship programme, which includes the Calor Village of the Year® for England and Wales competitions and the Calor Scottish Community of the Year® competition. Founded and developed by Calor to celebrate and reward those villages making a contribution to community life and encouraging rural sustainability, the Calor Village of the Year® competition is celebrating its tenth anniversary in 2006. It provides a substantial prize fund of over £39,000 at national level, but more than the monetary awards, villages benefit because the competition acts as a catalyst – encouraging people to work together and engendering a real sense of community spirit.

The Calor Village of the Year® for England competition judges villages on a variety of community issues with categories covering Community Life, Business, Young People, Older People, the Environment and Information Communication Technology (ICT). In addition to the national competition, which is administered and funded solely by Calor, Calor also supports county competitions in every county in England, from which entrants to the national event are drawn.

Since the competition began in 1997, over 300 villages have gone through the national judging process. Each one, win or lose, has reaped enormous benefit from the experience. A typical comment from participating villages, echoing a common theme at both county and national level, has been, 'We didn't realise so much went on. Taking part has helped us revitalise our community.'

For further information regarding the Calor Village of the Year® competitions, visit www.calorvillageoftheyear.org

St Neot is an isolated village on the edge of Bodmin Moor in Cornwall that is bursting with community spirit! Its 400 residents are not afraid to rise to a challenge and, more than that, enjoy coming together to achieve their aims.

As a result the village was a regional winner in 2002 and then scooped the overall title in the 2004 Calor Village of the Year® competition.

St Neot excelled in all areas of the competition; however, judges were particularly impressed with the 'Doorstep Green' – an area to cultivate wildlife and hold village events, created with over 2,000 hours of voluntary labour from villagers.